Preacher's A–Z

RICHARD LITTLEDALE

Illustrations by John Paterson

SAINT ANDREW PRESS
EDINBURGH

To the fellowship of Teddington Baptist Church –
who have enjoyed the blessed sermons and endured the not-so-blessed –
with thanks for their fellowship.

First published in 2008 by
SAINT ANDREW PRESS
121 George Street, Edinburgh EH2 4YN

ISBN 978 0 7152 0853 3

British Library Cataloguing in Publication Data
A catalogue record for this book is available from the British Library

It is the publisher's policy to only use papers that are natural and recyclable and that have been manufactured from timber grown in renewable, properly managed forests. All of the manufacturing processes of the papers are expected to conform to the environmental regulations of the country of origin.

Typeset by Waverley Typesetters, Fakenham
Printed and bound by Bell & Bain Limited, Glasgow

Contents

Foreword   vii

Introduction   ix

The A–Z

    A is for anointed   1

    B is for biblical   7

    C is for Christ-centred   13

    D is for dangerous   19

    E is for embodied   25

    F is for faithful   31

    G is for genuine   37

    H is for hwyl-driven   43

    I is for illustrative   47

    J is for juxtaposed   53

    K is for kinetic   59

    L is for love   67

    M is for mimetic   73

    N is for numinous   79

    O is for organic   85

    P is for pneumatic   91

    Q is for quickening   97

    R is for rhetoric   103

    S is for structured   109

T is for teamwork 115
U is for unfinished 121
V is for vulnerable 127
W is for wholehearted 133
X is for x 139
Y is for you 145
Z is for zeal 151

Before you preach 156
Preparing to preach 164
When you preach 180
After you preach 186
Bibliography 195

Foreword

Anyone who travels the streets of London knows it's easy to get lost. The first time my family visited the United Kingdom, I picked up a copy of Bill Bryson's *Notes from a Small Island*. I laughed out loud as he described asking directions from some gentlemen in a pub, only to be given three entirely different options, any one of them sufficient but, when piled on top of each other, utterly confusing. Then I experienced it at first hand in the Underground. The uniformed worker had just finished naming all the lines and stops to my destination, which I was dutifully memorising, and then he added: 'Or you could take the Jubilee and get off at …'. Anyone who travels the streets of London knows it's easy to get lost.

Anyone who travels the streets of the city called Preaching knows it's easy to get lost as well. How many different thoroughfares are there between text and pulpit? How many roundabouts as we decide between a word from Genesis as opposed to 2 Corinthians, and how does one ever get out of a roundabout? How many twists and turns between the pages of 2 Samuel and Luke? And soon the light will turn green, because Sunday is always coming and we will have to decide upon our course. How does one get to the pulpit from here? Stopped at an intersection marked Exegesis and Illustration, which way should we turn?

It was Charles Haddon Spurgeon who claimed that, in the same way that he could get to London from any hamlet in England, he could get to the cross from any text in the Bible. How does one get to the cross in the sermon? How does one not get lost in the midst of the city called Preaching? Richard Littledale's volume could be the preacher's new best friend, a companion on the journey, tucked away in our desks like a copy of an A–Z under our car seat. Of course, what makes his advice on a variety of homiletical topics so helpful is that he's been there before, in the pulpit and in the literature. Happy travelling, and may the Lord be with you!

PROFESSOR MIKE GRAVES
William K. McElvaney Visiting Professor of Preaching
and Director of Continuing Education,
Saint Paul School of Theology

'A written sermon is only 26 letters strategically arranged, but the possibilities are endless'

(Graves, *The Fully Alive Preacher*, p. 142)

Introduction

On a rainy night in 1935, jobbing artist and society girl Phyllis Pearsall found herself on the streets of Belgravia in London, utterly lost. It wasn't as if she weren't well travelled. The daughter of a Hungarian map-maker and an Irish-Italian painter, she had lived in England until 1920, when her parents' divorce led to her living alone in Paris, sometimes even sleeping on the streets. She had then returned to England in 1926 and spent a number of years travelling round Europe with her new husband. Now alone again, by the time she had found the street she was looking for on that rainy night, the party was over. Resolved that this would not do, she spent the next year working eighteen-hour days and logging some 23,000 of London's streets on foot in order to compile her A–Z. At first, no publisher would accept it, so she launched her own company and printed 10,000 copies. Her first order, for 250, was personally delivered to the newsagent by wheelbarrow! Years later, the A–Z brand is known the world over, and it is still the tried and tested companion of many a traveller.

While I cannot claim to have Phyllis Pearsall's skill or to have pounded the streets with her degree of vigour, the pages that follow are nonetheless the product of 'walking the road'. It has been my privilege to preach in many places and many different contexts. Sometimes this has been in large congregations, and sometimes in tiny gatherings. On occasions, it has been in a foreign language or through the kind help of a translator. It has certainly been quite a journey, and along the way I have been able to learn from others' wisdom and my own folly! You will find here a mixture of theology and common sense, practical advice and spiritual inspiration. Like preaching itself, this is a mixture of the earthly and the heavenly. In the end, my aim in writing these words has been not dissimilar to Ms Pearsall's. On the journey of preaching, I don't want anyone to get lost – whether preachers or listeners!

Like its illustrious namesake, this book can be used in a number of different ways:

To find a location. Most people turn to the A–Z because they want to get to a particular destination. They have heard its name, and may even have a rough idea of where to find it. However, it is precise directions they need. You may want to use the pages which follow in exactly that kind of way. If you want to know something about structure, or Bible basis, or zeal, then simply turn to the relevant chapter.

To browse. You can live in a great city for many years and still not get to know half of its streets and alleys, nooks and crannies. It is quite possible to while away hours simply looking at the intricate detail of an A–Z map and understanding the streets it depicts. If you have some time on your hands, why not browse through the pages of this book, flicking backwards and forwards as you do so? Some of what you read will be familiar, but you might also stumble upon the odd road or pathway which you never knew existed! Occasionally when I am looking at a map, I just have to go back and look at a strange street name. The same applies here. What on earth is the hwyl, and what has dye manufacture got to do with preaching? (You can find the answer to that one in the chapter on juxtaposition.)

To revisit. Years ago, in my first pastorate, I worked as an assistant to the hospital chaplain in our local hospital. It was interesting work, though stressful too. Some patients just needed some company, while others were seriously ill and feared for their lives. On one occasion, I met a long-term patient who had a set of maps spread out on his bed. When I asked him what he was doing, he explained that since his physical condition no longer allowed him to travel, he was using the maps to revisit all the places he had been in the past. As his finger traced the different roads and railway lines, so his mind travelled through all the experiences associated with them. If you are a preacher of many years' standing, why not use these pages to help you revisit the places on your preaching journey? Perhaps they will bring to mind the ups and downs you have known on the way. Based upon your own experience, you will probably start compiling your own alternative A–Z.

These days, the humble map seems to be under threat from GPS. Often a person will phone me from the car, only for our conversation to be interrupted by the monotone voice of the machine on the dashboard saying when to turn left or how far until you turn right. Like most automated systems, this is fine until the unpredictable occurs and things go wrong. In the end, there is no substitute for having a good map – and an even better map-reader to go along with it. On a long journey, I would rather have a map-reader and a map with me any day rather than a machine. The questions and insights in this book will be of most use if you engage with others about them. Talk about them, question them or even rewrite them – but, whatever you do, don't turn off the road!

Especially for those who are new to the preaching journey, you will find some additional help at the back of the book. Assuming no prior experience, the chapters after the 'Z' will take you from blank page to pulpit to feedback. They are not, of course, proscriptive. Over time, you will develop your own preaching style, and the voice which God has given you will find its own unique tone. That, however, is another story . . .

A is for anointed

A is for anointed. Not 'appointed', which you may have a mind to be; nor for 'admired', which you may one day hope to be; nor for 'awful', which you hope not to be. No, A is for anointed. Preaching begins with anointing, and ends without it. Without it, preaching is indistinguishable from any other form of monologue speech. It is the anointing of God which transforms the preacher's words from the ordinary into the extraordinary, the earthly into the heavenly.

Anointing in the Old Testament

There is much evidence in the Old Testament that the Israelites, like other ancient peoples round about them, made use of anointing. It was used for setting apart implements for special usage, such as the bowls and lamps in the temple for worship, or a mighty warrior's shield for battle. Equally, it was used for setting apart individuals for a special and public role. Every priest was anointed to their sacred task, and it was expected that a prophet should carry the anointing of God if he was truly to speak on his behalf. Perhaps the most well-known example of this 'anointing for purpose' is to be found in the story of the prophet Samuel anointing the boy David as king (1 Samuel 16:1–13). From the moment that the oil pours from Samuel's horn onto the teenage shepherd's head, he is deemed to carry the authority of God for his royal role. It is for this reason that Samuel was fearful to perform the anointing, with another king still on the throne. It is also for this reason that the reigning king fears the young pretender the most. From that moment onwards, despite his many failings, he carries the blessing and authority of God with him wherever he goes.

Anointing in the New Testament

In the New Testament, the most obvious example of anointing is Jesus Christ himself. His Jewish title 'Messiah' means 'anointed one' – and he demonstrates his anointing in words of heavenly wisdom and acts of unearthly power. From the moment of his baptism by John, he publicly carries a divine authority with him – like that carried by priests and prophets of the Old Testament, but of an entirely different order. When it comes to ordinary people, there is a great democratisation of anointing in the New Testament. From Pentecost day onwards, ordinary Christian men and women can expect to be touched by the Spirit in a way hitherto reserved for prophets and kings alone. This is the heart of Joel's prophecy, cited by Peter on Pentecost day: 'In the last days, God says, I will pour out my spirit on all people. Your sons and daughters will prophesy, your young men will see visions, and your old men will dream dreams' (Acts 2:17).

In every case, the anointing is evidence of God's special plan and intent towards the individual concerned. There are also special instances where the act of anointing is a way of marking an individual out for God's attention, as is the case with the anointing of the sick in James (5:13–15).

So, how does all this apply to preaching in the modern era?

Preacher

For the preacher himself or herself, there is a sense of honour and privilege of standing in a long line of those specially set apart by God stretching all the way back through the apostles of the early Church to the prophets of old. Like all of them, he or she has been selected by God for a holy and vital task. This is an honour. However, there is a flipside to this. Not only does a divine anointing mean that God expects great things of the preacher, it also means that he or she is incapable of performing them without God's equipping and blessing. As Jesus said: 'apart from me you can do nothing' (John 15:5). In the same way that an anointing conferred an invisible blessing on a pot or a lamp for the temple of old, so it does on the preacher. An unanointed pot is just a pot, and an unanointed preacher is just a maker of noise. An awareness of our anointing as preachers keeps us firmly in our place!

Congregation

Because of its importance in the Old Testament, there were severe punishments for people who did not take God's anointing seriously. Anyone caught using anointing oil for ordinary purposes, for instance, was liable to punishment. This means that preaching should not be treated lightly by those who listen to it. Before them stands a man or woman anointed by God for the purpose of speaking his words. Seen thus, the Sunday sermon is not a beauty parade, an alternative to Sunday-morning television, nor a theological equivalent of *The X Factor*! In appointing the preacher to the task, on a continuing or even an occasional basis, the congregation is calling on God to anoint him just as surely as Samuel did with David. The congregation sends the preacher into the jungle of the text and expects him to come back with something for them. When he does so, albeit scratched and bleeding from the expedition, they had best take him seriously, for he carries the anointing of God.

In my study, I have a small bottle of olive oil which I use on very rare occasions for anointing the sick. I'm not sure what it originally contained, but it certainly now has this holy purpose. The trouble is, it is so small! When I tip it up to pour oil over my fingers and onto the head of a sick person, the vacuum created in its tiny neck is so great that I am lucky to get anything out at all! Such a stingy anointing will not do at all for the preacher. If we are to attempt this sacred task of applying the Word of God, if we are to stand before the open mouths of his people and hope to feed them, we certainly need anointing. The trouble is, we need it by the bucketload and not the thimbleful!

B is for biblical

When I first became a Christian, there was a rumour in our (admittedly adolescent!) circles that you could tell a Christian by the size of their Bible. The bigger the Bible – the greater the Christian. In this peculiar view of spirituality, the preacher was expected to carry a Bible with gilded edges, a leather cover and dimensions big enough to flop over either side of his hand when he held it aloft to preach.

While it is entirely reasonable to expect a preacher to preach from the Bible, merely holding the Bible in his or her hand or even quoting from it extensively does not mean that the preaching is biblical. Holding a Bible in my hand when I preach no more makes me a biblical preacher than holding a baton in my hand would make me a conductor. In church settings where we expect the Bible to be quoted, or at least alluded to, in the sermon, we have been lulled into the false belief that such preaching is biblical. If we listen a little harder, we will see that some preaching may involve the Bible, or mention the Bible, without truly being based upon it.

Bible-biased

In this style of preaching, the preacher is essentially treating the congregation to an exposé of his or her views on a given subject. Those views are the product of many things, including life experience, character, personal history and conviction. In among the influences is some biblical input. To this extent, the view or the theology expressed is biblically biased. However, since it is not the only influence, it is dishonest to pass it off as biblical preaching per se. We often hear this kind of preaching when a preacher deals with a contemporary news story or event. Because the preacher is shaped by the Bible, their view on that event inevitably carries a biblical bias. However, that is not to say that the event and its implications are analysed under the microscope of biblical scrutiny. Rather, they are aired in the biblical setting of a church with the kind of biblical allusions you might expect there.

Bible-buffed

In this style, there is even less attempt to claim biblical authority for what the preacher is saying. Instead, we are given a clearly argued presentation of his or her point of view which is lightly dusted with biblical references in order to give it the appearance of biblical authenticity. Thematic preaching is particularly prone to fall into this trap. Out of the best of intentions, a preacher researches a particular theme in order to expound it for the congregation. Not surprisingly, it is to the books on the relevant subject that the preacher has turned – he or she can no more be expected to know what Christians say about every subject than a doctor can be expected to know about every ailment. As the preparation and writing progresses, the results of this research begin to form the body of the sermon. Then, as Sunday looms closer, biblical verses are inserted in order to authenticate the research. Is this biblical preaching?

Bible-bolstered

In this style, there is almost no attempt to preach from the Bible. Instead, the preacher expounds their particular theme based on their own research and conviction. If the Bible is referred to at all, it is only in order to bolster an argument already made on some other basis. The Bible clearly plays second fiddle to the preacher's own views and opinions. Where biblical allusions are made, it is often without precise quotations or references, but tends to be along the lines of 'the Bible says so too'.

Biblical

Truly biblical preaching is preaching where the Bible infuses both the language and the argument of the preacher. There is constant dialogue under way between the preacher's concern and the Bible's truth. In fact, it is more of a trialogue, where the Bible, the preacher and the world meet each other in the sacred space of the sermon. We could think of this in spatial terms. The preacher does not stand in front of the Bible, obscuring it with his or her own arguments and preferences, or stand behind it, saying so little about the biblical text that the congregation are left no wiser than they were before. Instead, he or she stands beside it – pointing out its features, allowing its beauty to shine, and making connections between it and the world all around. What follows is a pattern I have adopted for many years in the preparation of preaching. Each stage is explained below. You will notice also that each stage is 'interleaved' with prayer. There can never be too much prayer in the preparation of preaching. It is sobering to think that Billy Graham, a preacher who has addressed more of the earth's population than any other person alive, reckons on spending at least two hours in preparation for every fifteen minutes in the pulpit.

- *Read without*: your first impressions of the Biblical passage are your freshest. They come to you without any interference from other minds. Make a note of them – even if you modify them later.

- *Read with*: make use of commentaries in order to help you understand the passage. They will help you to understand obscure words and phrases, historical allusions and connections with other parts of scripture. Try to avoid the overly devotional commentaries, as they may go too far in telling you how to interpret the passage.

- *Write for*: now you are ready to start writing your sermon. But – remember that you are not writing it for just anybody. You are writing it for the particular group of people to whom God has called you to preach on this occasion. Perhaps you should imagine their faces before you in the study, just as a great radio broadcaster imagines their typical listener in the studio.

- *Pause*: this is a vital stage. If you can draft your sermon early on in the week, so much the better. This allows it time to 'percolate' – for the biblical imagery, language and ideas to invade your imagination. Never underestimate the value of this stage in the process. A pause in preparation, like silence in worship or white space in print, can be a vastly underrated asset. When you come back after your pause, it may look or sound different.

- *Read for*: now try to put yourself in the congregation's shoes. Try to read it with a critical mind as if someone else other than you had written it. How does your sermon sound? Does it make sense? Does it encourage you or challenge you? Is there anything in it which is too complex, or which draws too much attention to you as a preacher?

- *Preach for*: you notice that I do not say preach 'to'. It is a fine distinction, but a necessary one. We do things 'to' inanimate objects or supine people. We do things 'for' neighbours and friends.

- *Leave*: the word has left your heart, like a bird flying the nest. It is no longer your responsibility. Don't worry about it, fiddle with it, fish for compliments about it or regret it. God will take it on its onward journey without your help.

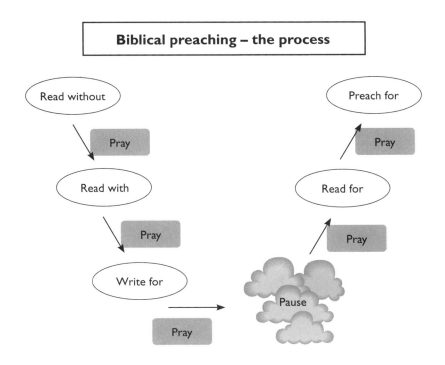

Biblical preaching – the process

Read without

Pray

Read with

Pray

Write for

Pray

Pause

Pray

Read for

Pray

Preach for

C is for Christ-centred

You will discover that, during the course of this book, there are a number of diagrams and illustrations of one kind or another. The diagram below is one that I have used on numerous occasions. Often, when I am speaking to a new Christian or an enquirer, a piece of paper and a felt-tip marker will come out, and I will draw the diagram again. In the simplest possible terms, it explains how the Bible fits together. All of the first 'half' is looking forward to the cross – in other words, to the birth, death and resurrection of Jesus Christ. All of the second 'half' is looking back on those events, whether from the immediate perspective of the gospel-writers or from the more distant one of the letter-writers. Meanwhile, there is a constant forward momentum towards the end of all things. As preachers, we would do well to bear this chart in mind.

Keep the Christ perspective

Remember where it is all leading, in terms of the Christ perspective. All scripture is, in some sense, the Word about Christ. This comes out in different ways in the different books and genres.

History

In the earliest history books of the Bible, we are introduced to the fall, which would eventually lead to the arrival of Christ. Even in the earliest seeds of rebellion, the first hints of salvation are expressed. In the words of the curse to the snake, the *proto-evangelium*, or promise of the virgin birth, is expressed (see Genesis 3:15). Elsewhere in the history books, we learn about the sacrificial system, which establishes the principle of costly forgiveness; and there are even hints of substitutionary death through the stories of young Isaac and Jephthah's daughter.

Poetry

As well as expressing the heart's yearning for God, the Psalms also have a lot to say about the need for forgiveness through sacrifice. They whet an appetite which only Christ can fulfil. In addition, there are overtly messianic psalms such as Psalm 22, where the physical details given about Christ's death several centuries before it happened are eerily accurate.

Wisdom

To many, the wisdom literature is a closed book. However, even here, there is a longing for someone who can encapsulate the personality and the wisdom of God himself. Every description of the true and righteous life points towards the incarnate life of God in Christ.

Prophecy

Much of the prophecy has a multiple focus. It focuses at once on the prophet's immediate situation, the eventual arrival of the Messiah, and the final return of the Messiah in glory on the Day of the Lord. In the overtly messianic prophecies, such as the servant songs of Isaiah, the focus on Christ could hardly be clearer.

Apocalyptic

This kind of literature, whether in Old Testament or New, has a distinct focus on the end of all things. However, here once again, there is much written about the radiant person of the Messiah. In the Old Testament apocalyptic of Daniel, for instance, we are given hints about a perfect God-man, such as Christ would be. In Malachi's Old Testament apocalyptic, and John's vision of Revelation, the focus is much more on the day of Christ's return in glory to judge the living and the dead.

Gospels

In the gospels, the focus on Christ is obvious, although all four provide it from different points of view. Mark's is a very raw perspective, written by one of the immediate circle of disciples. Matthew brings a particularly Jewish perspective. Luke's gospel is heavy with a sense of privilege and inclusion, since he was 'brought into the circle' at a later stage through the ministry of Paul. John's is different yet again, orientating his gospel for a world of mixed philosophies and religions where all the ancient certainties were under threat.

Letters

Obviously, there is great variety among the letters. They range from words of advice, such as 1 and 2 Timothy, to practical Christianity such as James, to applied theology in Romans and Philemon. However, their one unifying feature is that they all seek to apply the remarkable words and actions of Jesus in the individual and corporate life of the disciple.

Keep it in perspective

Although it is important for us as preachers to see the focus on Christ throughout scripture, that does not necessarily mean that every sermon is 'all about Jesus'. The Christ perspective which we have described above should colour our preparation more than it dominates our presentation. In fact, if we shoe-horn every sermon into an exposition of the role of Jesus, we may end up riding roughshod over scripture rather than respecting it. As we have said in the previous chapter, we need to allow the Bible to speak rather than putting words into its mouth. A congregation listening to a sermon on the third plague of Egypt and hearing an exposition of the life of Jesus may 'smell a rat' even while reading about gnats!

Preach Christ

As a preacher, you are called many things – including a mouthpiece and a fool! However, you are also called an ambassador. As Derek Tidball says in his excellent book *Builders and Fools*, 'Pastors should be clear that as ambassadors for the gospel they are called to preach Christ' (p. 16).

After reading that, I installed a new screensaver on my computer at work. On it, the words 'PC?' drift to and fro across the screen. As well as amusing my visitors, since it is obviously a PC, it serves as a reminder that, whatever else I am called to be or to do, I am called to preach Christ. The apostle Paul talks a lot about his preaching ministry, but perhaps the clearest definition of all is to be found near the beginning of his letter to the rebellious church at Corinth: 'we preach Christ and him crucified' (1 Corinthians 1:23). This should be a definition we can all apply to our preaching with honesty.

D is for dangerous

Many years ago, a friend of mine had a particularly wacky calendar. It was entitled 'Extreme Ironing', and showed people in various bizarre settings engaged in the rather mundane activity of ironing. Thus there were extreme ironers on the top of the Empire State Building, perched on the edge of the Grand Canyon, and perilously balanced on the ledge of Tower Bridge. The humour, of course, was meant to come from the comic juxtaposition of the ordinary and the dangerous. Some may feel that there is something equally comical about the very idea of preaching being dangerous. Isn't it, after all, the preserve of the mild-mannered and faintly ineffectual cleric?

The short answer, of course, is that it should be neither harmless nor ineffectual. In preaching, the voice of the living God thunders in human speech. Such an act should never be considered 'safe', in the sense of harmless, for either the preacher or the listener.

External dangers for the preacher

For the man or woman who feels called to speak up for God as a preacher, the dangers abound. There is ample evidence of this from the Bible and from the annals of Church history. Consider, for example, the case of Jeremiah. Many regard him as one of the finest Old Testament prophets. He has a sensitive heart and a flair for dramatic presentation which would be the envy of many a preacher. However, his honest proclamation brings him into such outright conflict with the 'official' prophets that he ends up spending a night in the stocks, exposed to public ridicule and shame. No wonder he emerged from them the next morning cursing the day he was born and the preacher's fire which burned within him.

The Lord Jesus Christ himself didn't fare much better. When he preached his first sermon in the synagogue in Nazareth, applying Old Testament scripture with devastating simplicity by saying that 'today in your hearing this prophecy is fulfilled', the result was far from positive. We are told by Luke that the seething mob hounded him out of the synagogue, drove him through the village streets, and all but lynched him by trying to throw him from a high cliff at the edge of the village (Luke 4:28–9). This is hardly the kind of positive response most preachers look for on a Sunday!

When Stephen, a man 'full of God's grace and power' (Acts 6:8), seized the opportunity of his trial to preach a thorough exposé of the Old Testament prophecies regarding Jesus, it incensed his hearers so much that it effectively sealed his death warrant. Although the sermon provoked a strong response from them, which we might regard as a positive result for any preacher, their next move was to rush him out of the city and stone him to death. Preaching can be a dangerous business!

Such a provocative response did not cease with the end of the New Testament, either. Hugh Latimer, sometime Bishop of London and a chaplain to the court of King Henry VIII, resisted all attempts to make him tone down his preaching for the sake of the royal ears. In fact, he insisted that it was necessary since 'a drop of rain maketh a hole in the stone, not by violence but by oft falling. Likewise a prince must be won by little and by little' (www.newble.co.uk/xheroes/latimer). In the end, his unbending stance made him so intolerable to the royal court that he was burned at the stake in 1555.

Centuries later, in the violent setting of El Salvador, Archbishop Oscar Romero was a priest with a reputation as a fiery preacher. He constantly preached a message of peace in the face of violence, urging his fellow countrymen to lay down their arms and stop attacking one another. Knowing full well that such a message would probably cost him his life one day, he said, prophetically: 'if they kill me, I will be resurrected in the Salvadoran people'. His fears proved well founded, and he was gunned down for his views, as were many who attended his funeral. A preacher can be a target in a dangerous setting.

Internal dangers for the preacher

The dangers for the preacher, however, are not just outside the Church. Some of them are in the Church, and some of them are within the preacher himself.

It has become something of a cliché to talk about the preacher who 'listens too much to his own sermons'. However, there is a grain of truth within it. To stand in front of a group of people who give you their undivided attention can be a seductive experience. Before long, you can convince yourself that you are in fact the most interesting person they have ever met, and it is their inestimable privilege to listen to you. One of the reasons it can be unwise to use too much humour in the pulpit is that, for the preacher, there is the temptation to use it for the sheer buzz of seeing your power to elicit a response from your listeners. To yield to the temptation to make people either laugh or cry, just because you can, is to stray into dangerous territory for the preacher.

There is a little-acknowledged danger of seduction, too, for those listening to the sermon. There is a potent sexual attraction to a good man speaking powerful words in a holy setting. If you don't believe me, think about the number of cult leaders who end up straying into bizarre sexual partnerships with many partners. Alternatively, consider how many preachers have been brought down by sexual sin. It is often said that the most powerful sexual organ is the tongue – and, as a professional speaker, the preacher should beware.

Dangers for the listener

The call to discipleship is always a costly one, whether that is a call to change our habits, transplant our lives, or in some corners of the world to *die* for our faith. For every listener to every sermon, there are significant dangers. To expose yourself to the razor-like quality of the Word of God, which 'is sharper than a two-edged sword' (Hebrews 4:12), is likely to have drastic consequences. People who have listened to sermons have finished up leaving their old life behind, yielding their possessions, abandoning their careers and more besides – so listeners beware!

E is for embodied

In the beginning was the Word. As we know, the timeless Word was made flesh in the person of Jesus. In human words, and with human gestures and actions, he made God manifest to men and women, which had never happened since the dawn of time. After his ascension, over the course of the next fifty to eighty years, the flesh was made word again as the gospel-writers recorded their memories of him. Since then, every preacher has sought to make that Word live again as he or she gives it voice. In this sense, all preaching is sacramental, since it makes God present through something ordinary – in this case, the preacher's physical presence and voice. Far from being a disembodied voice, the whole point about preaching is that it is God's Word expressed through the medium of human speech and the particular human life from which it emerges.

This means that there are real disadvantages to translocal ministry of the kind exercised by preachers who travel endlessly from one conference or rally to the next. Since they do not have to live cheek by jowl with those to whom they preach, this can encourage a somewhat cavalier attitude to what they say. Words can be tossed out from the platform or pulpit without the preacher having to work through the nitty-gritty business of applying them in the lives of those who listen. Furthermore, the congregation is never given the opportunity to scrutinise the preacher's life in order to see if the words are being lived out by him or her. While many local pastors will testify to the incredible burden which this embodied preaching ministry lays upon them, few would be without it either.

If we once accept this concept of preaching as embodied Word, it has some very specific applications to our preaching ministry. It may affect everything from our diet to our vocabulary and our wardrobe!

Diet

Since your voice is your God-given instrument, you must look after it just as carefully as a violinist might cherish her Stradivarius or a sprinter might care for his legs. Avoid smoking, for a start, since you cannot afford to affect the quality of your voice. You should also avoid any foods or drinks which tend to give you a dryness of the mouth or a tenderness to the throat. For some, this means that their preparation to preach on Sunday morning may begin with choices made on a Saturday evening: will I drink a second glass of wine, or should I eat that really hot curry? In fact, it goes beyond Saturdays and Sundays. As a preacher, are you looking after your body as well as you can? If God had wanted to communicate by speaking from the skies or writing in the clouds, he would have done so. The fact is, he did not! Instead, he has chosen people like you to embody the Word every time you preach. This means that the care of our bodies is both a spiritual and a professional discipline.

Posture

In some ways, this is related to the above, since it concerns our physical presentation of the Word. This was brought home to me when I began to train as a preacher. Despite my many years in acting and theatre, the college's speech therapist picked up straight away that I was habitually leaning to one side as I spoke in order to minimise my height. Her words 'stand tall for Mr God' still ring in my ears every time I preach! Our posture when we preach should express neither threat nor self-importance. However, we should be careful, too, that, in a bid to convey informality, it does not suggest a casualness towards the Word of God itself. As an embodied message, your body language will be read by listeners to see whether you really believe that what you are saying is important.

Dress

In his book *One Hit Wonderland*, Tony Hawks describes a particular preacher he encountered on his travels, wearing a crumpled brown suit and drab tie. He describes him as 'Quite a picture, but not one you'd buy an expensive frame for' (p. 31). A preacher in crumpled, grubby clothes, preaching about the meticulous care of God in creation, may well find that the medium and the message conflict with each other! The main thing to bear in mind when choosing what to wear when you preach is that it should not be the thing that people remember about the sermon. In other words, they should not remember what you wore either because it was too dressy and drew attention to you, or because it was so scruffy that they were left with the impression you did not take the task seriously.

Vocabulary

Of course, our vocabulary should be a genuine reflection of who we are, as we shall explore in the chapter on 'Genuine'. The concern here, however, is that it should be the kind of vocabulary befitting the embodied Word. This means that any kind of humour which relies on belittling or dismissing others is completely unacceptable. Scan your language for any trace of racism or sexism. Furthermore, language whose only intention is to impress the listener and bolster the intellectual prowess of the speaker should be discarded. Preachers should also pay careful heed to the warnings in James chapter 3 about those who would preach. He reminds us that, all too often, we use our one mouth for both good and ill: 'out of the same mouth come praise and cursing. My brothers, this should not be' (James 3:10). There is a real danger that, if we swear and use abusive language outside the pulpit, at some point it will weaken our ability to embody the Word inside it. 'Getting away with it' from Monday to Friday, as far as language is concerned, is a myth. Our tongue needs to be constantly yielded to God, and not just when we preach.

A friend of mine, who is an outstanding musician, recently won an international composing competition. His prize is a bespoke trumpet – fashioned to his exact specifications. He has chosen the metal from which it will be made, the exact configuration of the valves, and even the inlay on the valve keys. It embodies his personality, and once it is in his hands I know that he will make it sing. If God has chosen to embody his Word through your voice, who are you to argue? In his hands, you will sing too – provided that you let him work through you.

F is for faithful

Some years ago, it was my privilege to teach at two residential workshops in northern India on expository preaching. The audiences at each workshop were highly attentive and very keen to learn. For the most part, the participants appeared to go away encouraged and uplifted. However, after one session, an earnest young man with a long face came to see me. He explained that he had been doing his best to abide by the principles I was teaching in his church. He was praying, preaching and pastoring as best he could but seeing no tangible fruit. Was he doing anything wrong, he wanted to know? Of course, I knew very little about his situation, but I explained the biblical principle of faithfulness rather than fruitfulness. In both versions of the parable of the talents, there are rewards for those who yield a profit, regardless of its size. In essence, it is faithfulness rather than fruitfulness for which the servants are rewarded. At this, the young pastor went away reassured.

As preachers, we rely upon this principle of faithfulness rather than fruitfulness. This does not mean that we settle entirely for a faithful but fruitless ministry. Indeed, if such a state of affairs persists for long, we should ask ourselves serious questions. However, the *first* question we should always ask ourselves is: 'am I being faithful?' If the answer to that question is 'yes', then we must start to look at what fruit (if any) is growing. As we do so, we should remember that the images of growth in the New Testament are all associated with biological or horticultural growth – none of which happens overnight! A preacher who is struggling to see fruit may need to address his or her technique. A preacher who cannot see faithfulness when he looks in the mirror needs to address his heart.

Faithful to your calling

When God calls a man or woman to speak up for him, he accords them an enormous privilege. Rather than communicating through signs, wonders and portents in the heavens, he has chosen at this time to communicate through you and your voice. No wonder that people like Moses and Jeremiah in the Old Testament and Paul in the New felt a sense of awe at their call. It is for this reason that we are permitted such a close-up view of the story of their call, since it would be so often repeated in the centuries which followed. To be faithful as a preacher means constantly maintaining an awareness that God in his peculiar wisdom has called *you* to carry out this task for him.

Faithful to your congregation

A wise pastor often used to ask aspiring preachers the following question: if you feel called to preach, does anyone feel called to listen? The fact is, the people who have asked you to preach, on either an occasional or an ongoing basis, *do* feel called to listen to you. They are giving you their time, which is limited, and their undivided attention, which is precious. If you are to be faithful to them as they put their faith in you, you must put in the hard work required. They have a right to expect you to seek God in the anguish of prayer and seek wisdom in books in order to prepare a sermon for them. It is to this task that they have called you. Be faithful to them, and honour them, not just in the public space of the pulpit, but also in the private space of the study.

Faithful to the Bible

As we saw in our second chapter, biblical preaching does not just mean peppering your sermon with dozens of biblical quotations. It is far more fundamental than that. Being faithful to the Bible in preaching means allowing it to challenge the ideas you had before you approached the text. It also means ensuring that the finished product after your preparation of the text is faithful in content, tone and teaching to the text from which it sprang. Would the author of the chosen Bible passage recognise it as inspired by his handiwork, or at least be prepared for it to go out under his name? A sermon should never clash in fundamental theology, or even tone, with the passage from which it was drawn. When sermon and passage grate against each other, the preaching cannot be said to be faithful to the Bible.

Faithful to the Spirit

The Holy Spirit is the breath of God which allows us to make a God-inspired sound, just as the breath of a trumpeter allows his trumpet to sound the call to battle or the first note of a symphony. In order to be a faithful preacher, we must be prepared to heed the Spirit's voice during both the preparation and the delivery of the sermon. This is the case even when his instructions may seem unexpected or bizarre. There may even be occasions when we end up like Paul in Acts 16:7, where the Holy Spirit 'keeps' us from speaking. On other occasions, our faithfulness to the Holy Spirit may mean that we appear unfaithful to the notes we prepared so carefully in advance, or even that we break faith with the people to whom we preach – having to tell them harsh truths. As difficult as this may be, remember that a preacher unmoved by the Spirit is like a trumpet with no breath in it – empty and lifeless.

Faithful to the end

Faithful preaching, shaped by the Holy Spirit and the scriptures, is a hard task to fulfil. However, having once received the call of God to do it, we must be faithful in pursuing it. This will require a soft heart, a thick skin and a humble spirit. We must resolve to be faithful to the task as long as we are called to fulfil it. The great musician Roy Castle was interviewed on television shortly before his death. Asked what his greatest concert ever had been, he replied that he 'hadn't played it yet'. Perhaps you haven't preached your greatest sermon yet. Perhaps you won't preach it this side of heaven. Since none of us knows when that day will be, the best thing is to keep preaching faithfully as long as we have the calling and the breath to do it.

G is for genuine

Way back in the mists of time, sailors used to bite down on the gold coins with which they were paid in order to make sure they were genuine. After all their hard labour, they did not want to be fobbed off with a thinly disguised piece of lead. No, they wanted the genuine article. The same is true when it comes to preachers. While people don't tend to perform the bite test, they nonetheless want to be sure that their preacher is genuine. Does he or she really mean what they say? In this age of political spin, people are more wary than ever of messages which have more skill than substance, and are rightly sceptical about presentation over content. Of course, this doesn't mean that you shouldn't pay careful attention to your presentation, as we have already seen. However, your words must be honest and genuine through and through. If they are not, then (a bit like the bite test) people will find out in the end – and it is likely to hurt when they do! Years before political spin was formally invented, Professor Karl Barth was teaching preaching in Germany, and later in Switzerland. He wrote some very profound material on the theology of preaching, but also some practical and down-to-earth advice for his students. He warns, for instance, against the danger of borrowing another person's ideas, or style, and passing them off as your own. With characteristic flair, he describes this as 'posturing in borrowed plumes' (*The Preaching of the Gospel*, p. 52).

Some practical advice of my own follows.

Avoid false emotion

Genuine emotion is one thing, and we shall deal with it under the headings of H and V. Artificial emotion, however, is quite another. If you raise your voice in an attempt to sound passionate when you do not feel it, no-one will be fooled. Equally, if you make the pretence of grief or sadness when you do not feel it, you are likely to undermine not just this sermon but many subsequent ones too. Tears are precious in the sight of God and his people, and should never be shed, or even suggested, for effect. In the Orthodox tradition, tears are seen as a sign of the Holy Spirit's descent on an individual. Any preacher tempted to claim tears as a weapon in his or her armoury might do well to remember that.

Avoid false humour

Am I the only sceptic, or are you instantly suspicious when a preacher claims that 'a funny thing happened to me'? Also, the statement that 'the story is told' instantly makes me feel that maybe it isn't. Genuine, life-affirming, observational humour can be to the sermon like the seasoning to a meal – really bringing out the flavour. When the humour is laboured, however, it has quite the opposite effect. If the funny story you are telling did not happen to you, then don't claim that it did. If something is meant to be funny and you think your listeners will find it funny, but it leaves you cold – don't, for goodness' sake, laugh just to give them the idea. You'll probably put them off! A preacher who laughs too heartily at his or her own jokes is a liability.

Avoid false knowledge

It is absolutely vital for preachers to study the language and culture of the people to whom they preach. This should be done just as carefully as a missionary might do it in a far-off land. You need to find out all about the books your congregation read, the films and television programmes they watch, the music they listen to and the newspapers they take. In time, this will allow you to speak their language, thereby shortening the communication distance between pulpit and pew. There is the world of difference, though, between taking an interest and claiming to be an expert. A preacher who watches one episode of a soap opera in order to plunder it for illustrations is on a par with a call-centre operative on the other side of the world who does the same in order to sound British. In other words – unconvincing! By all means, watch the programmes your listeners watch in order to identify with them. Over time, you may grow to enjoy them, and you will then find that you can illustrate from them with ease. However, the preacher who tosses in illustrations about the performance of the local football team when he never watches them, or the fate of a soap-opera character which he only got second hand from a newspaper, is likely to be rumbled before too long. Preachers beware!

Before we leave this subject of genuine preaching, there are two other points to mention. The first is the question of whether genuine preaching means that we are rendered unable to preach in times of personal suffering. If we are to be utterly genuine in the pulpit, does that mean that we cannot preach when our heart is breaking or our spirit is troubled? I do not believe that it does. In fact, my personal experience has been that the discipline of preaching through a crisis often produces a sermon which is sharp and hardened – like steel tempered in the flame. Kirk Byron Jones, in his fascinating book *The Jazz of Preaching*, on the relationship between preaching and jazz music, draws a parallel here with blues music, which arose out of great suffering: 'When it comes to preaching through times of emotional strain and pain the question is not how to preach when your heart is not in it. The question is how to preach with a different heart, a wounded heart' (p. 20). Can we preach through times of trial and still be genuine? As long as we preach different sermons, we certainly can.

The second point is the claim often made that a congregation can only progress as far spiritually as the preacher has gone himself or herself. Anything else, it is claimed, is false and hollow. This argument, I believe, not only condemns us to lives of spiritual mediocrity but also misunderstands the preacher's task. The preacher, surely, is to cry 'follow him' rather than 'follow me'? Yes, preachers must be genuine in all they say and do, even if this means admitting that faith and belief is a struggle. However, this does not mean that the congregation is obliged to struggle too. A voice of faith raised in the wilderness of suffering can still point out the way of the Lord – even if the one doing the shouting is not able to take that way just now.

H is for hwyl-driven

In the early part of the twentieth century, a spiritual revolution was starting in the hills and valleys of Wales. Beginning with acts of repentance at small evangelistic meetings, it spread like a forest fire until whole communities were engulfed. In the end, tens of thousands of men and women became Christians. Preaching was important for all those involved with the revival, although it reflected the different backgrounds and practices of those involved. While dissenting preachers laid a heavy emphasis on doctrinal accuracy, Methodists set a lot of store by authentic experience. It is out of their particular tradition that the hwyl arose.

Some describe it as the word for 'sail', while others describe it as the kind of whoop uttered by followers of cock-fighting when their bird is winning! It encapsulates that moment when the preacher becomes so caught up with his theme that the Spirit of God seems to carry him along, like the wind filling the sails of a huge sailing ship and sending it skimming across the waves. During the revival, a particular feature of this was that the preacher would move from an ordinary speaking voice into a kind of song, where he would begin to intone the sermon in an almost sing-song way. Each preacher would have his own distinctive tune, and when he moved into it he was said to be preaching 'with the hwyl'. At the time, this was a moment of high excitement among the congregation, as they felt that the power of God was moving in their midst.

For many today, the revival is a distant memory recounted to them by their grandparents, and the sound of the hwyl is rarely heard. However, it has survived as a word in other contexts. In that combination of Welsh and English spoken in the valleys and referred to as 'Wenglish', a man is said to be 'in his oils' (hwyls) when he is doing something he really enjoys. People observing such a person would see a man with an unself-conscious enjoyment and absorption in what he is doing, rather like the preachers of old caught up in their theme. In rugby stadia, even outside Wales, many a rugby coach may urge his players to capture 'the hwyl', enabling them to outstrip their average ability and play with unstoppable passion.

The hwyl for you

As you will read in other chapters, manufactured emotion or passion does not deserve the name of preaching. If we were to work ourselves up into a lather in the pulpit and begin to sing our closing points in order to recapture the power of the revival, the most likely outcome would be the congregation's derision! The image of the sailing ship, however, is very powerful. Hours of work have gone into its construction; a crew of dedicated sailors are aboard and ready to sail it. It is a beautiful, majestic thing, but entirely lifeless until the wind fills its sails. Keep that picture in your mind next time you enter the pulpit or stand behind the lectern. All your preparation and study is no more use than the construction of the ship in the dry dock – until and unless the Spirit fills you like the wind filling the sails. As a young Christian, I was very influenced by the writing of the American pastor A. W. Tozer. His book on a life of spiritual pursuit, entitled *Leaning into the Wind*, is well thumbed by now. On its cover is a picture of a ship in full sail with its sails stretched by the power of the wind. Whenever I preach, I want to be that boat. To be hwyl-driven in your preaching is to be acutely aware of your reliance upon the Holy Spirit. Not only that, a hwyl-driven preacher also comes to the sermon with something of the excitement we feel when a ship slips its moorings for the start of an adventurous journey. Of course, the ship has been carefully prepared and the charts have been read, but ahead lies an exciting voyage with the prospects of high adventure and distant horizons.

A prayer

It seems like a long way from the valleys of Wales in the early 1900s to the city of Constantinople in the early 800s. However, perhaps the young bishop of that city was anticipating the arrival of the hwyl without even knowing it. I close this chapter with the introduction to his little book on the Spirit-filled life:

> You who desire to capture the wondrous divine illumination of our Saviour Jesus Christ – who seek to feel the divine fire in your heart – who strive to sense and experience the feeling of reconciliation with God – who, in order to unearth the treasure buried in the field of your heart and to gain possession of it, have renounced everything worldly – who desire the candles of our souls to burn brightly even now, and who fear for this purpose and have renounced all the world – who wish by conscious experience to know and to receive the kingdom of heaven existing within you – come and I will impart to you the science of eternal heavenly life.
>
> (Prayer of Nicephorus, www.acts2024ministries)

I is for illustrative

Shouldn't that be 'illustrated'? After all, every sermon needs illustrations like a house needs windows. They let the light in and allow the occupants to see the world outside. Illustrations are one of the preacher's devices to ensure that Word and world have something to do with each other. That said, some illustrations are so murky and overused that they let little light in. Rather, as a friend of mine used to say, they are like old windows: difficult to shut up, easy to see through, and always a pane! The availability of illustrations online, cross-referenced and thematically arranged, is definitely a mixed blessing. Too many preachers seem to fish in the same pond for their illustrations – and the same old stories come out again and again, like the same old boot on the end of every fisherman's line. Like the boot, they are not very appetising!

If you are going to use illustrations, there are two simple rules to observe.

Illustrations must illustrate

In other words, illustrations must not be inserted for the sake of variety, nor to 'pad out' the sermon, nor for any other reason than to illustrate a point. They will do this best if they are clearly germane to the subject in hand, and reasonably contemporary. I was brought up on Blondin the tightrope-walker as an illustration of faith – especially when he asked for a volunteer to be wheeled in a wheelbarrow across a tightrope over the Niagara Falls. In itself, it is a perfectly good illustration – but it all took place in 1860, which is now a century and a half ago! If we can't find other examples of risky faith, then we simply haven't been looking hard enough! Centuries ago, Martin Luther urged his students to keep an eye out for illustrations all around them – in the fields, in the town, in the home and even in the mirror. This was good advice, since it keeps us alert to contemporary rather than historical illustrations. It is not just the age of an illustration that matters, but also its content. Strange though it may seem, if an illustration is too absorbing or amusing or troubling, it may end up occupying the minds of the congregation for the duration of the sermon. Clearly, this is counter-productive! The illustration should assist the main thrust of the sermon, and never the other way round.

Illustrations must not be abusive

No preacher would willingly use an illustration which is abusive; but it is easy to slip into it without really noticing. If, for instance, the preacher illustrates from his or her private family life, or from a private pastoral conversation, he may well be abusing the privacy of those involved. Preacher, did your child give you permission to be used as a sermon illustration … or perhaps they were too young to do so? An illustration can be abusive, too, if it relies on the kind of humour which belittles or stereotypes any group – whether on the grounds of race, colour or gender. The other way in which preachers can misuse illustrations, abusing the good nature of the congregation, is by constantly illustrating their sermons from a source which is important to them but maybe not so important to the congregation. I have slipped into this myself on returning from trips to the Church overseas. Those intense experiences may be very important to me, but if I share them too much they become exclusive and shut out those who did not share them. The same might be said of any illustrations which are always drawn from the same source – be it a film or a football team. In the end, such illustrations may end up illustrating little more than the preacher's obsession.

We turn now to the ways in which preaching can be illustrative, rather than just illustrated.

Illustrative of grace

As with many other parts of the sermon, illustrations can have perfectly good content which is then undermined by the tone in which they are delivered. As preachers, we need to take particularly careful note of Paul's injunction that our speech should be 'always full of grace, seasoned as it were with salt' (Colossians 4:6). This means avoiding any tone or any phrases which suggest superiority over the listeners. As a general rule, the word 'we' is always more appropriate than 'you' in preaching. It underlines how you stand level with those who listen rather than over them. In this way, the sermon should be illustrative of how it is possible to apply the Word of God with authority into lives and situations without being authoritarian. Can you give vent to your passion and conviction, can you articulate your learning and study without hectoring those who listen to you? Preaching should be illustrative in that it should demonstrate correct and appropriate handling of the Word of God. It was for this that Paul urged his young apprentice, Timothy, to strive. He was told to 'present yourself to God as one approved, a workman who does not need to be ashamed, and who correctly handles the word of truth' (2 Timothy 2:15).

Illustrative of persistence

Preaching should be illustrative, too, of the ability to persist under pressure. Many preachers carry considerable burdens in addition to their preaching. Ordained ministers have all the concerns of church and pastoral life to bear, while lay preachers often balance their preaching with busy working lives. As well as all this, preachers have children to feed, families to visit, elderly parents to care for and health concerns. Particularly in a local context, the congregation will be aware of some of these issues. As they listen to the preacher, they will be asking questions not only about how they are coping, but also about the impact of the Word of God when life is tough. Illustrated in the preacher, for good or ill, will be the applicability or otherwise of the Word of God in adverse circumstances. In other words, does it still ring true 'when the chips are down'? This can be the toughest test of all for any preacher. However, it is also one of the most obvious ways in which the power of God can be demonstrated. Years ago, I was preaching through the book of Nehemiah with some students in the former Yugoslavia. As the week went by, many students received their call-up papers to go and fight in Kosovo. Those who had not yet received them were expecting them at any minute. One morning, I levelled with them and said that 'this is either relevant now, in these circumstances, or it is never relevant at all'. The sessions which followed were among the most captivating in which I have ever participated.

Illustrative of handling scripture

A good sermon should not just explain a portion of scripture, but should also provide the tools and skills for people to explore scripture for themselves. Preaching should illustrate such good techniques of Bible study that people are empowered and enthused to do it for themselves. This is one of the reasons that I always encourage those who listen to have a Bible open in front of them. Although this can have other less positive consequences (see the discussion of the 'Shakespeare syndrome' in chapter 'V'), it can have real positive gains. When people interact with the written Word while you are preaching on it, they are more likely to forge connections which will remain after the sermon itself is over. In other words, if you want to preach a sermon which lasts seven days (in its effect rather than its duration, of course), you need to illustrate how to handle scripture in the way that you preach. Some disciplines jealously guard their expertise in order to protect the status of the expert. This should not be so in preaching. If people go away from the sermon knowing more about the passage simply because you told them, and more convinced than ever about your expertise, you have failed. When you are assessing a sermon's worth, always ask yourself not just what it has illustrated about scripture, but also what it has demonstrated about the business of understanding scripture.

J is for juxtaposed

In a factory in France in the eighteenth century, experiments were under way in the Royal Tapestry Works which would affect not only the colouring of dyes for the royal houses but also the insights of science and the progress of impressionist art. As dye-maker in chief, the young chemist Michel Chevreul was keen to produce dyes of the brightest possible hues, so that they would not only look spectacular when first woven but also stand the test of time. It was during this research that he made his breakthrough discovery. Two skeins of different-coloured wool, when held next to each other, would make a brighter hue than if the two dyes had been blended in the first place. In other words, a skein of red and a skein of yellow wool, held next to each other, would make a brighter orange in the eye of the beholder than a single skein of orange-dyed wool. When painters like Seurat, Pissarro and Signac got hold of this idea, they began to create canvases with extraordinary life and vitality, as dots of pure single colour were juxtaposed and set the picture dancing with brilliant colour.

As preachers, it is words we wield, rather than brushes; but Chevreul's principle can still serve us. By juxtaposing different truths and different words, we can create more vivid pictures in the minds and more lasting impressions in the hearts of our hearers than we might otherwise have done. Our aim, of course, is not just to *show* the Word of God but to impress it upon those who listen.

Let's look at how this principle of juxtaposition might help us to do so.

Preacher and people

Physically, you stand opposite each other – you occupy different spaces. This is true whether you hold your church in the round or in some more traditional format. However your worship space is arranged, there is nonetheless a difference as you stand and speak while they sit and listen. In this, you see before you on a Sunday a parable of what has happened throughout the week. You have moved in different circles, faced different issues and jumped different hurdles. This need not be a bad thing, though. So long as you are honest about the differences, there is no reason why this particular juxtaposition should not be as creative as Seurat's brush. The congregation sends you into the Word, and you send them into the world. They approach the Bible from the world's perspective; you approach the world from the Bible's perspective. You have spent the week worrying about their souls and soothing their wounds; they have spent the week earning your salary and keeping you in prayer. Much of your week's activity has been dictated by the needs of the church, while much of theirs has been directed by the needs of their employers or their families. When you come to the act of preaching, you both come to it from different places, like actors entering the stage from different wings. This can only be a good thing. *Vive la différence!*

Word and world

Of course, there is a big gap between Word and world too. The Old Testament was written in the days when half the world was not known to exist, and God was sometimes treated as a national totem. The New Testament was written in the days when Rome thought it ruled the world, and many in northern Europe still lived a tribal and relatively primitive existence. Modern translations and contemporary language should not blind us to the fact that the Bible emerges from a different world to our own. Not only are there these historical differences between Word and world, but also there are gigantic spiritual ones. The Bible's perspective is entirely focused on the first and second coming of Jesus, as we have seen in chapter 'C'. The world's perspective is focused elsewhere, whether that be in the selfish realms of profit, the noble cause of peace, or the doomsday concentration on the depletion of the earth's resources. As we juxtapose these two in the pulpit, each throws the other into stark relief, like a jeweller producing a piece of black velvet on which to display his most perfect diamond. Within the sermon, there should be a constant interplay between the Bible's view and the world's view. Each should highlight the other, like dots of pure colour dancing before our eyes. Each should interrogate the other, with the world saying 'is it really so?' and the Bible saying 'need it really be so?' Too many preachers embark on the fruitless quest to reconcile the Bible's view with the world's, and vice versa. It cannot be done, and indeed it *should not* be done. In his fascinating book *Peculiar Speech*, William Willimon points out the danger of this approach when he warns that we spend our time trying to make the gospel relevant to the world, when it should in fact be the other way round! A good sermon leaves the listener hungry to see the world differently, and the preacher hungry to read the Bible differently.

Here and hereafter

There is a popular cliché that preachers are always calling time on their congregations and reminding them that the end is nigh. While a constant concentration on that subject would certainly be an unbalanced diet, the preacher should nonetheless keep it in mind. Particularly where he or she is engaged full-time in church work, and therefore set apart by others to think about such things, there is a duty of care to continually draw people's attention back to the finite amount of time which remains. It may once have been true that some Christians were 'so heavenly minded that they were no earthly good'; however, in the Western church today, it is more likely to be the other way round. Our worldly preoccupations are so consuming that we are far more likely to forget heaven than we are to dwell on it too much. A preacher should constantly be flitting between the concerns of today and the promises of tomorrow, like Seurat's brush constantly dancing between the light and the dark on his palette in order to bring his picture to life. If you don't remind people as a preacher that heaven is waiting – who will do it? We must learn to juxtapose the cares of today and the promises for tomorrow with great skill if we are to bring the Word to life.

If you stand close to one of the great pointillist paintings, you will be very disappointed. All you will see is a random jumble of dots and splashes. It is only by distancing yourself from the painting that the mixing of the colours by your brain works its magic. As with many elements of preaching discussed in this book, you will find it hard to see for yourself whether you are putting it into practice. You will need to rely on trusted friends and advisors to tell you whether you are juxtaposing Word and world to bring the gospel into sharp relief.

K is for kinetic

On the night of the premiere performance of Handel's *Messiah*, the great composer mingled with people in the salon afterwards to receive their congratulations and discuss his great work. However, when one high-society lady announced that she had 'enjoyed' the performance, Handel's patience snapped. 'Madame,' he said, 'I did not write it for you to enjoy, I wrote it to make you different.' Many preachers who have undergone the 'nice-sermon-thank-you' encounter at the church door will know just how he felt. Preaching is not just about the transfer of information from one individual to a group. It is not about what people learn, but about what they become. A 'successful' sermon is not the one which has conveyed the most knowledge and understanding to its listeners. Rather, a successful sermon is one that has allowed an encounter between God and his people to take place. Scripture shows us that no-one, from Moses in the Old Testament to the apostle John in the New, comes away from such an encounter unchanged. Preaching is about changing people, making them different. Ultimately, preaching is kinetic – it is all about moving people from where they are to a place closer to God and further in towards the centre of his purposes.

Moving the individual

In those traditions where preaching carries a high status within the liturgical life of the church, it is nonetheless important to remember what it is *for*. This is equally true in those churches of an academic evangelical tradition, where the critical analysis of the sermon has become as much of a tradition as the Sunday roast. The sermon is not about exalting the written Word, nor about demonstrating the academic prowess of the preacher. Rather, it is a tool in the hands of God to shape men and women into the likeness of Christ. In terms of the individual, a sermon can be said to have succeeded if it has moved them on from where they were before they heard it. This may happen in a number of different ways. They may have a more profound understanding of a particular biblical passage or theme. They may find themselves more resolved to act upon what they already knew. They may find an insatiable thirst to pursue a particular topic or to read a particular Bible book in more depth. All of these things, only some of which are apparent to the preacher, are evidence that there is a kinetic energy in the preaching. As that energy is released, it is converted into action, either mental or physical, in the life of the listener.

Moving the church

All that we have said about the kinetic effect of preaching in the life of the individual should be 'writ large' in the life of the church. Particularly in those churches where one person provides the bulk of the preaching diet, it should be possible to ascertain the kinetic impact of the preaching upon the church. Is it more loving, more active or more spiritually energised than it was before that particular preaching ministry began? This is not to say that the preaching ministry alone is responsible for changes in all those areas. To believe that would be both arrogant and foolish. However, it would be equally foolish to believe that preaching did not have a contribution to make towards the church's growth in grace. In fact, if it did not, would there be any point in doing it, much less in learning to do it better? Preaching should be kinetic because it releases the energy of God's Word into the corporate life of the church, which is then translated into movement on the road of service. Preaching which confirms the church's stationary position in the lay-by is of little help to the Kingdom. On the other hand, preaching which puts fuel in the tank and keeps the church moving is worthy of the name.

Moving towards the end

Many years ago, as a wide-eyed and impressionable teenager, I attended a huge international mission gathering in Switzerland. Young people from all over Europe gathered together, slept on thin foam mattresses and flocked to central meetings in Lausanne to hear international speakers sound the clarion call for mission. One particularly memorable message was the one based on Christ's words in Mark 13:10 that 'first the gospel must be preached to all nations'. The speaker's clear implication was that, once we had achieved the task of preaching the gospel to every single ethnic group on Planet Earth, then Jesus would return. While I would now want to question his analysis of the passage, he nonetheless taught me a very valuable lesson. All preaching, indeed all ministry, is conducted with the insistent sound of a ticking clock in the background. The ministry of the Word is one means of moving people towards their final encounter with the Living God and ensuring that they are ready for it. When the final day comes and all the books are opened, we will see how much our preaching has done to fuel the missionary fire and to incline the soul towards eternity.

Moving the preacher

If we are expecting our preaching to move the congregation and the individuals who comprise it, we should also expect it to move the preacher. Anyone who has ever prepared biblical material for presentation to others, whether that be in a Sunday school or a university seminar, will know that they learn at least as much for themselves as they pass on to others. It is wise for the preacher to recognise and indeed to celebrate that process. The longer we go on studying the Bible in order to present it to others, the deeper our understanding of it will become. Not only that, but also our deeper understanding means that, on subsequent occasions when we read the same passage, we bring new questions to it, and so the process continues. This is like a spiral of energy in which the preacher is driven on in a quest for greater understanding. You can see this in graphic form in this figure. We should look for this particular kinetic energy in our lives as preachers; and, if it is missing, then we need to pray for its swift return.

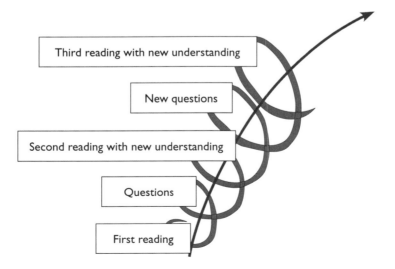

Third reading with new understanding

New questions

Second reading with new understanding

Questions

First reading

Moving preachers

While we are on the subject of kinetic energy and movement, we need to touch on the subject of moving preachers. This is not a reference to those preachers who bring an (intentional) tear to the eyes of their congregations. It is instead a warning about the dangers of too much movement while in the act of preaching. While it is good to avoid a posture which is so staid that it becomes boring, we should also avoid the kind of restless energy and pacing which distracts the listener from the message itself. Some preachers move about so much that the listeners end up sharing what appears to be their discomfort. Instead of applying their minds and hearts to the words that are said, their eyes are doing all the work as they follow the preacher up and down and round and round the platform on his or her restless journey. Although this kind of movement is often associated with a relaxed and informal style of preaching, we have to recognise that it may not be relaxed for all those who listen. We need to guard, too, against the kind of repetitive or extravagant gestures which draw undue attention to themselves. It is a good idea to ask a trusted friend to video you when you preach, and then to watch the video with them at a later date. You will be amazed at the number of repetitive gestures you make, and particularly at the number of times you touch your face when you speak. These things are all force of habit; but, like most habits, they can be unlearned if the incentive is sufficiently great. In this case, it surely is, since we want to communicate as effectively as we can for the sake of the gospel.

Hold this book tightly in your hand now. Squeeze its pages tightly between your fingers until your knuckles begin to change colour. Can you feel it moving? Can you feel the constant buzz of the molecules which make up its pages? Of course, you can't. However, it is true that all solid matter is in fact moving all the time. It is the constant movement of the molecules in perfect tandem with one another which creates the impression of a solid mass. God has built movement into the most fundamental laws of the universe – so why should there not be movement in our preaching too?

L is for love

Someone once described the act of preaching as 'twenty minutes in which to love the congregation'. I wonder how many of those involved with preaching, either by doing it or listening to it, would agree with the description? In a culture where preachers speak uninterrupted for their allotted time, it is possible to do all sorts of things with these twenty minutes. They can use them to harangue the congregation, to propound their particular theological or political views, or even to address particular agendas with members of the congregation. None of these could properly be called preaching.

To deal with the last point first, the pulpit should never be used to say things to members of the congregation which you would not be prepared to say face to face. Sadly, this does happen occasionally, especially when a pastor feels embattled and criticised. The pulpit is the one part of his (or her) ministry where he still feels in control. Knowing that he will not be contradicted for the entirety of the sermon's length, he uses his preaching time to say those things to his detractors which he would fear to say in any other setting. This is unacceptable on a number of counts. Firstly, it makes improper use of the authority of the preached Word, clothing a personal agenda in spiritual dress. Secondly, it fails to address the needs of those who are not caught up in the preacher's particular dispute. They have a right to expect that they can come to church and hear a Word of God to address their particular situation. Instead, they are treated to the preacher wrestling his personal demons! Thirdly, his calling as pastor demands that he put the spiritual well-being of his flock first – even when they are out to get him! Of course, these underlying personality issues do have to be dealt with in order to maintain the unity of the fellowship. However, the pulpit is not the place to do it.

Preaching as love begins in the study, or more properly on the knees. It is because you love the people to whom you preach that you will pray and wrestle and agonise and cry out in order to find the right Word for them. No preacher should ever be content to preach a sermon that 'will do'. Before you ever begin the process of preparation, you should seek the Lord for the needs of this particular group of people at this particular time. This is the case even when you are tied into a lectionary or other preaching scheme. Because you love these people, you must still call on God to tell you how exactly you should approach the subject, how precisely you should tackle the passage in hand for the sake of these people whom you know and he loves. Think of Solomon, crying out for help when he first acceded to the throne of his father: 'I am only a little child and do not know how to carry out my duties. Your servant is here among a people you have chosen, a great people too numerous to count or number. So give your servant a discerning heart' (1 Kings 3:7–9).

If possible, have a picture of your church or congregation before you as you pray. Better still, if there is a local vantage point where you can look down on the church and community whom you serve – pray there. Think of Abram looking down on the city of Sodom and interceding for it.

Preaching as love continues now into the serious business of preparation. Your love for these people dictates how hard you study for their sake. It also affects your particular choice of vocabulary and your approach to the passage or subject. You are not preaching to impress your homiletics teacher. You are not preaching to win plaudits. You are not preaching to convince these people of your brilliance as a biblical scholar. You are preaching only and always because you love them. If you find yourself choosing a particular phrase because it will impress people – think again. If you find yourself inserting a particular reference to prove that you have been studying hard – take it out. Love is the grammar of preaching, dictating how it is put together and how the recipients make sense of it. Rushed preparation at this stage suggests a lack of love on your part, and may turn the honey of the word to a bitter taste in the mouths of those who receive it. A friend of mine used to say that the food she cooked tasted inferior if it was not 'cooked with love'. The same could be said of preaching.

Because preaching is love, you arrive at the church in plenty of time in order to preach. A flustered preacher rushing in at the last minute without the time to pray or collect his or her thoughts is not showing true love towards the congregation. The sacrifice of time which you make is part of your love towards them. Of course, there are other things which you must do without – be it an extra half-hour in bed or the time for another cup of coffee. However, if you love these people, you will not mind giving them the time, just as you would not mind spending time to travel to a friend's wedding or to cook a meal for your family. Be careful, too, that you do not make a habit of complaining while preaching about how long and arduous the preparation has been. Do this once too often, and you will end up sounding like a person who complains about how much a gift cost them when they hand it over!

The other sense in which preaching is love is that you should love to do it. Of course, if you are employed full-time by a church, there is an aspect of duty to your preaching. You have agreed to preach the Word whether you feel like it or not. However, despite all the work and effort involved, your heart should beat just a little faster at the prospect of preaching your next sermon. Like an athlete limbering up for the next race and training long hours to be ready for it, or like Jeremiah who has the Word of God 'in my heart like a fire, like a fire shut up in my bones' (Jeremiah 19:9), you must love to preach, or people will not love to listen. If you are to be a truly great preacher, loving your congregation and winning their love in return, then the fire of love must burn within you.

M is for mimetic

'Mimetic' is not a word we use very often, unless we are fans of Richard Dawkins and his theories on memes. In his groundbreaking book *The Selfish Gene*, he explores among other things the concept of memes – ideas which float around through history and are passed on from generation to generation in much the same way as genetic material is passed on. This is the process of mimesis. However, the idea that we learn to say the things which others have said before us and do the things which others have done before us is hardly new. It certainly finds a place in biblical literature. We are told that, throughout his stormy years at the helm of God's people of Israel, Moses constantly had young Joshua at his shoulder – watching, listening and learning. The apostle Paul positively encourages this technique when he urges the rebellious Corinthian church to 'imitate me as I imitate Christ' (1 Corinthians 11:1). Jesus underlines the power of example when he looks up from washing the disciples' feet and says: 'I have set you an *example* that you should do as I have done for you' (John 13:15). The word he uses for 'example' is *paradigmo*, from which we derive 'paradigm', and which in modern Greek describes the dotted outline you might draw for a child to follow as they learn to form their first letters.

This process of imitation takes place just as much in preaching as it does in other areas of Christian service. David Schlafer describes the witnesses who are always present when we stand up to preach. 'They will not step forward to introduce themselves, but they are present, and they are not silent' (*Your Way with God's Word*, p. 33). We are all under the influence of others when we stand up to preach – whether consciously or unconsciously. The question is what we should do about our preaching models.

Acknowledge them

The first thing we should do with these influences is to acknowledge them, both to ourselves and others. Have a listen to a representative sample of your recent sermons, or read the scripts of them. Can you see certain influences emerging? You might hear the voice of your first pastor, recognise the tone of your Sunday-school teacher, or even see shades of your parents. Bear in mind that, if you can see these things, there are undoubtedly others who can too. This need not be a bad thing. There is certainly no need for you to feel frustrated or embarrassed. In fact, it is far better to acknowledge those influences to yourself and others. When I was first considering the Christian ministry, I worshipped in a Baptist church in a university town. The pastor of that church had a congregation which ranged from the local roadsweeper on the one hand to the vice-principal of the university on the other. His easy manner and accessible vocabulary were a model in communication skills. To this day, I am sure that his influence is to be heard in most of the sermons I preach.

Shake them by the hand

If we are to go the whole way in acknowledging the influence of others upon our preaching, then we should seriously consider telling them about it. Obviously, if your key preaching influence has been Martin Lloyd Jones or John Calvin, you will have to wait until you get to heaven in order to tell them about it! However, if it was the minister of your first church or your Sunday-school teacher or your theology lecturer, why not stop reading this right now to go and tell them? While it is a biblical principle that we shape each other's lives, it is also a sound principle that we thank those who have helped us. It is to this end that Luke records the story of the ten lepers, and it may also be behind Paul's injunction that a person who benefits from another's preaching should 'share all good things with his instructor' (Galatians 6:6). To thank those who have shaped us not only helps us to be honest about where our preaching came from but also recycles the encouragement around God's Kingdom.

Choose them

Having acknowledged the influences on your preaching thus far, and having gone out of your way to thank them where you can, now it is time that you started *choosing* the influences upon you. There are numerous sources to which you can turn. Within the Bible, you could look to the fiery and impassioned preaching of Peter, or the closely argued reasoning of Paul. You might choose to dwell on the poetic style of Jeremiah or the rich stories of Jesus. Within the Christian tradition, there are many great collections of published sermons to read. However, since preaching is an oral act, it is important that you supplement the diet with recordings or podcasts of other people preaching too. This is especially valuable when they are from people who have written about preaching, such as Thomas Long or Fred Craddock – that way, you can listen to check whether they 'practise what they preach'! You may want to look, too, to other sources. Who are the politicians or other public communicators whom you admire, and why? If you can learn something from their command of the language, or their passionate energy, or their presentation skills, don't be afraid to do so. You may not agree with any of the content of what they are saying, but their means of saying it could teach you a lot. Since we know that preaching is mimetic, or learned, we need to make sure that there are plenty of people from whom we learn. If possible, make sure that you don't just read books of preaching, but books of speeches too.

Become one

Although you will go on learning and being shaped throughout your preaching life, recognise that you will also start to become an influence upon others. They will learn not only about God from you, but also about preaching itself. Although this is a weighty responsibility, it is also a great honour. I shall never forget the occasion when I revisited my first church and enjoyed the preaching ministry of a young man in his late teens. It had been my privilege a few years earlier to baptise and disciple him. Now he stood in the pulpit preaching a passionate and convincing sermon which warmed my heart. If there was something familiar about the tone of his voice and the shape of his phraseology, perhaps I should not have been surprised. Many years on, he has doubtless developed a style all of his own; but I am honoured to have been part of the process.

N is for numinous

As we have already said in our chapter on juxtaposition, we should avoid being so earthly-minded that we are no heavenly good. As preachers, we must avoid being too earth-bound and prosaic. People who come to church expecting a brush with the holy have just as much right to expect it in the sermon as they do in any other part of the service. In fact, since so much of our perception of the world is shaped through language, they may even have a right to expect it more.

It is hard to pin down the definition of 'numinous'. It is a word which was first coined by Rudolf Otto in his book *The Idea of the Holy* in 1923. Derived from the Latin word *numen* (meaning 'spirit'), it is used to describe those aspects of holiness which have nothing to do with our rational being or our moral behaviour. When we spontaneously drop our voices on entering a vast cathedral, when we gasp at the majesty of God's creation in a spectacular view, or even when we find ourselves grinning uncontrollably in response to exuberant praise songs, we may be said to be having a numinous experience. In what ways can we expect preaching to contribute to this aspect of our spirituality?

Language

Although the days are gone when preachers were household names because of their charismatic presence and their command of language, that is no reason why we should not aim for the best. We should plunder the resources of language and literature in order to come up with words and phrases which describe the indescribable, frame the infinite for all to see, and set the imagination tingling. This does not mean that we should opt for language which is either self-consciously flowery or hopelessly obscure. What it does mean is that we should take time in choosing our vocabulary when we preach. Since we are often trying to describe things which are beyond words or are so spectacular that they are almost beyond our imagination, we should not opt for the first and most prosaic word which comes to hand. Consider this snatch of Paul's prayer for the Ephesians: 'And I pray that you, being rooted and established in love, may have power, together with all the saints, to grasp how wide and long and high and deep is the love of Christ' (Ephesians 3:17–18).

It is hard to believe that those words simply flowed effortlessly off his pen. I wonder how many false starts or crossings-out there were before he finally came up with such a captivating way of saying 'I hope you realise how much Christ loves you'? Look also at some of the spectacular descriptions of nature in Job, the Bible's oldest book. Phrases such as the dawn 'taking the earth by its edges and shaking the wicked out of it' (Job 38:13) or the 'storehouses of the snow' (Job 38:22) are designed to set the imagination alight.

Ideas

It is not just how we talk that matters, but also those things which we choose to talk about. While it is probably true that some preaching is so rooted in the biblical world that it bears no relation to the one in which we live, it may be that the pendulum has swung too much the other way. In a bid to provide preaching whose practical application is obvious and whose relevance to daily living is high, many preachers have shied away from the more mysterious aspects of our faith. If a topic cannot be demonstrably put into practice in the office or the playground or the family tomorrow, it is left to one side. Such preaching stands little chance of generating a truly numinous experience. Furthermore, it may be very short-sighted. Crudely put, it may give us something for tomorrow but leave us starving for the day after tomorrow. Of course, preachers should tread cautiously around those subjects which they struggle to understand. Of course, they should never lead their congregations into mysteries of such depth that their only accomplishment is to get everybody (themselves included) lost. However, there is something about the human make-up which means that human beings need mystery in order to function. As preachers, we should not be afraid to tackle those ideas which we cannot fully explain – such as the nature of heaven or the gap between death and resurrection. It may not be our job always to explain, but sometimes only to highlight or point out. When we do this, we may find that people are attracted inexorably towards these less explicable aspects of God, like Moses kicking off his sandals and walking towards the burning bush.

Horizon

Preaching which concentrates always on the mundane, and which rejects any insight which cannot be put to practical use tomorrow, may end up spectacularly missing the point. As preachers, we always have our eyes on the more distant horizon, and should preach accordingly. I was once asked to describe my job in a live radio interview. Without the time to think about it properly, I responded that I was 'coaching people for heaven'. Although it was an instinctive response, I believe that it captures something fundamental about the preacher's task. Through our prayer and study, and the preaching words which they help us to produce, we are preparing those who listen for an eternity in the presence of God. Strange though it sounds, there is a sense in which our job as preachers is to get people ready to die. If our preaching does not touch on aspects of faith to do with eternal living, we shall have failed.

Places and pulse

In his fabulous book *Finally Comes the Poet*, Walter Brueggemann reminds preachers that preaching is not all about instruction: 'The deep places of our lives, places of resistance and embrace, are not ultimately reached by instruction' (p. 109).

If we want to connect people with the numinous aspects of their faith, it is those 'deep places' which we must target. This means that we must keep our finger on the spiritual pulse of our congregations. What are they really worried about? Which aspects of their faith do they struggle hardest to grasp? Which promises have they taken to heart, and which ones have slipped through their fingers? To find the answers to these questions takes hours of prayer and lots of time listening to people, but it is incumbent on us as preachers to put the effort in. Once we know how and where people's spiritual horizons are limited, we can then start to direct their gaze in appropriate new directions.

Pertinent questions

One of the things which keeps preaching mundane and robs it of the numinous is the feeling shared by many preachers that they must not raise in a sermon any question which they cannot answer. It is true that the use of questions can be abused in the pulpit. It can be a lazy short-cut to give the sermon a semblance of theological edge. It can be an unseemly way for the preacher to wrestle his or her personal demons in public. However, the proper use of questions can be entirely appropriate. A provocative question can ensure that the sermon lingers in the listener's mind long after the sermon is over. Indeed, this is a technique used by Jesus himself. Many of his parables ask more questions than they answer, and were designed to make people think about things they had never before considered. If we want to nudge people in the direction of the numinous, questions can be a good way of doing it.

If preaching is to serve its purpose as a 'live' word of God, there has to be a place for the mysterious in preaching. That said, we should ensure that the biggest mystery in preaching is *not* why anybody bothers to listen to it!

O is for organic

Although the word 'organic' is something we are more used to seeing on our fruit and vegetables in the supermarket than on our preaching programme, there is a sense in which all preaching is organic. By this, I mean preaching which recognises that God, preacher, Bible and world are locked together in a cycle whose purpose is growth and whose outcome is fruit. Within this, there is an organic bond, a relationship which runs far deeper than structure or formal process. This can best be explained by reference to the diagram on p. 86. Those of you who remember your science schoolbooks may well recognise that it is based on the water cycle. Below, each of the elements of the cycle is explained.

Players

People

The people in this cycle are rooted in the world and the Word. They are rooted in the world because they have no choice – by the forces of nature and the providence of God, this is where they were born. They are rooted in the Word because they have chosen it. At a given point, they have decided to accept it as an authentic word from God to humankind. They are in the church and under the ministry of a preacher because they believe that the Bible is,

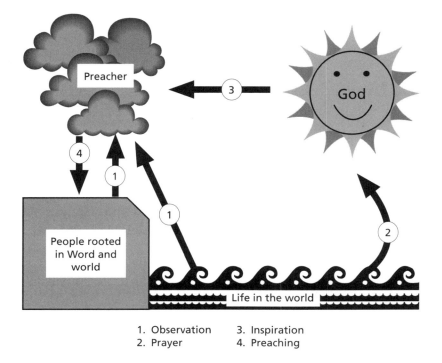

1. Observation   3. Inspiration
2. Prayer   4. Preaching

and can be, the Word of God. They approach it each week with a thirst and expectancy born of experience.

Life in the world

Whatever the people hear on a Sunday will wash off them and into their life in the world, like water running off a cliff and into the sea. It will affect their behaviour and their priorities. It will give a distinctive flavour to their life. Sometimes, it will be so diluted as to make scarcely any difference – like the rainwater trickling into the sea. Other times, it will propel them like a torrent into the world which begins on Monday – like an unstoppable river turning salt water fresh. The real test of preaching is to be found more on Monday than on Sunday.

God

God watches over the whole scene – like the sun shining on seas and dry land alike. He hears the prayers emerging from his children in the world, he listens to the preacher communicating on his behalf, and he sees the rainfall of his Word as it falls. Without the sun, the cloud cannot rise high enough to rain, and the moisture cannot evaporate from the sea. In the same way, God inspires the preacher while also drawing the prayers out of his people.

Preacher

The preacher sits close to the people, but in close contact with God himself. He or she is moved by the sun, is touched by the moisture from the sea, and gives of her- or himself to the land. The preacher sits on the cusp of land and sea – letting the rain fall on the land but watching to see how it affects the sea. A preacher looks for a Sunday response but longs for a Monday application.

Processes

1. Observation

The preacher is constantly observing his or her people. He or she observes them both in the church as they handle the Word, and in the world as they handle their calling. As the cloud draws its moisture from the rivers and streams and also from the sea, so the preacher draws his or her understanding from quiet pastoral observation. If you know lots about how your congregation behave in church, but little about how they behave in the workplace, then your preaching will suffer. Try to devote time not just to studying the Word, but also to studying these precious people whom God has entrusted to you. Your appreciation of them, and of the Word which you seek to apply to them, will grow as you do so.

2. Prayer

All the way through the week, prayers ascend to God from his people living out their lives in the world. They are praying for his help and looking for strength to live an authentic Christian life in the world. They may also be praying already for next Sunday's sermon – crying out for refreshment as the sea might cry out for rain.

3. Inspiration

Moved by the prayers of the people, and with an eye to the preacher, God provides inspiration. In the water cycle, the sun draws the moisture up from the sea, just as God draws the prayers of his people to himself. In the water cycle, the sun also warms the air, making the cloud rise to the point where it is 'ripe' to release its moisture as rain. God prepares preachers, raising them up and filling them with inspiration, to the point where they have a Word which can refresh and invigorate the people. Preachers often talk about 'preparing the sermon', both during the week and on the Sunday just before the sermon is delivered. However, in truth it is the preacher who needs to be prepared, rather than the sermon. As the cloud must reach the right 'texture' to rain, so the preacher must attain the right degree of humility before God and dependence upon God in order to be of any use in the pulpit. More sermons are undone by underprepared hearts than by underprepared notes.

4. Preaching

Warmed by the sun, saturated with the moisture from streams, rivers and seas, at last the cloud releases its welcome burden. The water pours down on the dry ground, refreshing every place it touches and running off into the waiting waters of the sea. Preaching should come as a release to the preacher and a refreshment to the listener. In a truly organic model of preaching, the sermon blesses preacher and listener in equal measure.

The hardest thing about describing the preaching process through this model is knowing where to start. Does it start with preaching ... or the praying ... or even the inspiration? Does it start from the preacher, or the people ... or from God himself? Of course, all are true. Like the proverbial chicken and the egg, none came either first or last. What it does show us, however, is the complete interdependence of the different elements. Without sun, evaporation or clouds, no rain falls and nothing grows. In this model, all the 'players' change, with the exception of God. Preachers may have different forms and styles, just like the different shapes of cloud. Life in the world will inevitably change, just as the levels of the sea rise and fall. People rooted in the world will change, just as the shape of cliffs changes over the centuries. And yet, the process remains the same.

If the experts are to be believed, organic food is good for us. It brings the kind of real nutrition that artificial foods cannot. If we want our preaching to be full of real goodness, we need to fix this process in our minds and hearts. (A fuller version of these ideas can be found in my *Stale Bread?*, pp. 227–35.)

P is for pneumatic

Back in the days of pre-digital cameras, I used to use an SLR camera with all the relevant kit and caboodle. In a large aluminium flight case, I carried a camera body, lenses, filters, flash gun and all the relevant accessories. This kit accompanied me to various places in Europe, and also to three weddings where I acted as official photographer. Often, people would peer into the case and comment on its contents. However, on all these occasions, there was one piece of kit which caused more comment than any other – my aerosol can of compressed air. Why, people asked, did I need a can of air, when the stuff was all around anyway? Of course, the point was that the can allowed me to direct that air with great power and precision to exactly the spots where it was needed in the complex mechanism of the camera. Even something as simple as air can be powerful when it is directed to the right place. Pneumatic preaching is all about the Spirit channelling his energy with great force and precision to those places where it is needed most.

Before preparation

Our reliance on the Holy Spirit in preaching begins long before a word is spoken, or even a note is written. It may be that you are responsible for choosing the subject upon which you preach. If so, you carry an awesome responsibility, and must ask for the Spirit's help as you bear it. The Bible tells us that no-one understands God's mind like the Spirit does, and that no-one can affect our minds like the Spirit does. 'For who among men knows the thoughts of a man except the man's spirit within him? In the same way no-one knows the thoughts of God except the Spirit of God' (1 Corinthians 2:11).

Expect the Spirit to direct you towards the deep-seated and well-hidden needs of the congregation which only he can meet. This will affect your choice of subject matter, your selection of biblical material and the initial approach of your preparation. It is important to develop this attitude of dependency upon the Spirit even if you are *not* responsible for choosing what to preach on. In those contexts where you are preaching through a lectionary or preaching schedule, you should be just as reliant on the Spirit to prime your initial approach to the preparation. Sometimes, you will doubtless be asked to preach in other churches, and told that you are free to select your own theme. What should you do? Contact someone in that church, whether it is the church warden, organist, minister or even the caretaker! Ask about what issues the church is facing and has recently faced. Ask about the spiritual 'temperature' of the place. Once you have all that information, take it away to a quiet place and dwell on it in prayer. Under the Spirit's guidance, this will help you to direct the Word of God with power and accuracy to those places where it is needed.

In preparation

Whenever possible while writing this book, I have done so with the door onto the garden open beside me. I like to feel the fresh air as I work, and once in a while a freak gust can certainly make life interesting as it upsets all my papers and rearranges them as it sees fit! Metaphorically speaking, you should always work with the window open. Always keep an ear open for God's word of caution, or stimulus, or challenge. One of the gravest dangers as we build up our experience in preaching is that we acquire an unhelpful degree of self-confidence. Bible passages, and even key themes, become very familiar. We can open a passage or look at a theme and tell at a glance what approach might be adopted. While this can be helpful in an emergency situation, where we are called upon to preach with little or no notice, it should not set the tone for our preaching ministry in general. Come to the passage or theme, instead, humbly relying on the Spirit's guidance. By all means use the biblical resources available, as we have discussed in chapter 'B'. However, it is absolutely vital that we keep alert for the Spirit's surprising guidance. You may have read a passage twenty times and preached on it ten, but don't be surprised if the Spirit steers you differently as you approach it for the eleventh sermon. In fact, you should probably be pleased!

In delivery

If there are two spiritual gifts that the preacher needs especially, they are the gifts of wisdom and knowledge described in Paul's Corinthian list. 'To one there is given through the Spirit the message of wisdom, to another the message of knowledge by means of the same Spirit' (1 Corinthians 12:8).

Definitions vary, but basically they denote that gift whereby the Spirit of God reveals to us things which we could not have known by purely natural means. Once in a while, the Spirit will reveal something to you while you are in the act of preaching which causes you to alter what you were planning to say. This may be a simple change in turn of phrase, or it may mean highlighting a particular need or situation. I experienced this on one particularly memorable occasion when preaching through the Ten Commandments. While preaching on the commandment not to kill, I felt an overwhelming conviction that I needed to mention abortion. In the church that night, unknown to me, was a visitor who had struggled for years with the associated guilt she felt from assisting at the termination of her sister's pregnancy. On hearing this specific word, she felt able to ask for prayer and counselling after the service was over. On other occasions, I have been prompted to adjust the tone of what is said. A stern warning has been modified to a cautionary word by the Spirit's warm breath, or a bland statement has been blown to the white heat of conviction through his mighty wind. Most preachers, no matter how long they have been preaching, will continue to experience a degree of nerves about doing it. They are not alone. Great preachers such as Martin Luther and Charles Spurgeon often felt so totally inadequate to preach that they were rendered all but speechless before mounting the steps of the pulpit. This is no bad thing, since it keeps preachers reliant on the Spirit's help. I am nervous every single time I preach, and turn on almost every occasion to Christ's reassuring words in Luke's gospel: 'When you are brought before synagogues, rulers and authorities, do not worry about how you will defend yourselves or what you should say, for the Holy Spirit will teach you at that time what you should say' (Luke 12:11–12).

The act of preaching is impossible without the Spirit, just as speech is impossible without breath.

After delivery

In some traditions, the preacher will close the sermon with the word 'amen' and a reverent bow of the head. In others, the preached word is followed by a reverent silence and an appropriate song. In others, the sermon's conclusion is signalled by verbal responses from the congregation. However, no matter what our tradition might be, there is an interesting question about when the sermon actually ends. Does it end when the last word leaves the preacher's lips, when that word reaches the listeners' ears ... or much later, when it reaches a person's heart? If it is the last, then the sermon may not end for several days ... or even weeks. Long after the church lights are turned off and the preacher has gone home to relax from this sermon or to write the next one, the sermon may still be doing its work. In this hidden phase of the sermon's life, the Spirit is just as much at work as in the others – or even more so. Pneumatic preaching is preaching which relies on the Spirit from beginning to end ... even when the end is hidden from view. As you will see in chapter 'U', this is a cause for celebration, because God's agenda is usually longer than the preacher's.

Q is for quickening

When I was first a Christian, I can remember being more than a little puzzled by the phrase in 1 Peter 4:5 that Christ would come to judge 'the quick and the dead'. Since I was always bottom in my year for PE at school, I sincerely hoped this did not mean that the slow would be left behind! Of course, 'the quick' in that particular context simply refers to those who are alive.

Preaching is never about creating life – which is God's job. Instead, it is all about encouraging and stimulating spiritual life where it is found in the hearts of believers. As we take his Word and apply it under the guidance of his Holy Spirit, our hope is to quicken the spirits of those who listen. It is like introducing a naked flame among newspaper and tinder in the fireplace, and then needing someone to blow gently on it to transfer the flame. Although we rely upon God for that truly supernatural act, there are nonetheless things that we can do in order to maximise the quickening potential of our preaching.

Keen observation

You need to live close enough to your people to see what God is up to in their lives on a daily basis. Without breaking any confidences, celebrate the breaking through of spiritual life in small and great steps. This might be a person learning to pray out loud for the first time, or a quadrupling of church income! Obviously, the Bible provides us with a treasury of stories about triumphant faith. However, we must not neglect the evidence of faith right under our noses. Where the preacher is also the pastor, that person is in a unique position to observe and to celebrate these signs of spiritual life. While it is incumbent on you to protect the identities of those involved, you can nonetheless make it clear that you are describing the lives and triumphs of people you have *actually* met. Not long ago, I had a visit from a new member of our congregation, who told me that her encounter with the gospel was changing not just the way she spoke (removing the swear-words from her vocabulary) but also the way she felt about everything. At the next Sunday's evangelistic guest service, I just had to share these words, without saying anything about the person who spoke them. People will believe in the power of the Word not just when they experience it in their own lives, but also when they observe it in the lives of others. It is on this basis, of course, that many products are sold – it worked for her, so why shouldn't it work for me? While this might seem like a lowbrow way to communicate God's Word, it is nonetheless true that people are crying out to know whether it works. Wherever it is possible to demonstrate that it does, we should do so.

Appropriate adaptation

Even where you are tied into a lectionary or preaching programme, there should still be scope for adapting and orientating material appropriately for your particular congregation. In her fascinating book *Preaching as Local Theology and Folk Art*, Leonora Tubbs Tisdale discusses the importance of setting our preaching within a cultural context in just the same way as a cross-cultural missionary might do. This can help us to find appropriate ways of targeting and phrasing our preaching. If we want to see God's Word quickening the spiritual life of the congregation, we must make strenuous efforts to adapt our approach and vocabulary to their particular setting. In addition to the aspects we have already discussed about books they read and programmes they watch, there is a historical element to consider too. A church, like a town, or indeed a family, has its own particular history. Events in the church's past will invest particular words and phrases, even particular aspects of our faith, with special meaning. If, for example, a church has suffered a tragic death, it will listen differently to sermons on suffering. If it has experienced marital infidelity from a person in authority, there will be an invisible wall of scepticism in your way whenever you broach the subject of leadership. None of these things is insurmountable. In fact, with sensitivity, the church can reach a particularly acute understanding of these things. It works the other way, too, investing different words and theological truths with positive meaning because of the church's good experiences. In my own church, our experience of a costly redevelopment programme has generated new understandings of God's provision and his inspiration to do great things. If your desire is to quicken the congregation through the preached Word, you will have to understand their history. This may take months, or even years, to achieve.

Self-giving

Often when we seek to bring or even to stimulate life, we must give of ourselves in order to do so. If you blow on a spark to make it into a flame, you give of your breath. Your life breath contributes to the birth of the flame. If you give mouth-to-mouth resuscitation to a dying person, you fill their lungs with your breath in order to save them. In the same way, if you want your preaching to have a quickening effect, you must be prepared to give of yourself – body, mind and soul. This applies in the act of preaching itself, but also in all the hours of preparation which lie behind it. You give of yourself listening to the stories of their triumphs and disasters. You give of yourself admiring their babies or holding their dying hands. You give of yourself laughing with them or crying for them. You certainly give of yourself as you cry out to God to fill them with his life, whether through your words or anybody else's. Preaching which brings life may take a lot out of the person who preaches it. Many of the most fruitful preaching ministries in the world have left those who exercised them all but worn out.

As preachers, our key text is God's Word of life, the Bible. We believe it to be a life-giving book. Unlike other books, which sow doubt or spread terror or appeal to our baser instincts, this book is life-giving. The question is whether our preaching enhances or masks that quality. It is often said that, while Jesus turned water into wine, preachers perform the feat the other way round and turn the rich wine of God's Word into insipid water. Look around you next Sunday – do you see evidence of life breaking out as the sound of God's Word is heard? If you do, you should rejoice and continue in faith. If you do not, you should redouble your efforts in the pulpit and quadruple your efforts on your knees. As preachers, it is easy to forget that God wants results even more than we do!

R is for rhetoric

At its most basic, rhetoric is the study of communication. Ever since Aristotle described it as a 'means of persuasion' and Plato as 'the art of winning the soul by discourse', fine minds have examined how best to touch mind, body and spirit to the maximum effect. Everything to do with the spoken word has come under the microscope – from volume and tone to gestures and vocabulary. Rhetoricians have assessed how speech, sound and gesture can be combined to maximum effect to persuade the listener. However, in Christian circles, as soon as you start to use words like 'persuasion', people get nervous. For some, any attempt at persuasion on the speaker's part smacks of manipulation on the one hand, and a failure to rely on the Holy Spirit on the other. This need not be so. If preaching is the act of giving voice to God's Word; if its intent is to reach the deep places of body and soul for the Kingdom's sake, then no communication stone should be left unturned. Obviously, we should not resort to anything which is dishonest or emotionally manipulative. Nonetheless, there are plenty of rhetorical devices at our disposal which can be put to good use in preaching.

Questions

Questions, whether rhetorical or requiring an answer from the congregation, are a powerful tool for the preacher. Because they engage the listener directly and require a response, they can be very useful in retaining the attention of those who listen. A long 'passage' of speech can be broken up with questions to ensure that preacher and listeners stay on the journey together. They help to ensure that preaching, though largely a monologue, can still be a participative act. It is important, however, that the questions are carefully phrased. There is nothing more uncomfortable for a congregation than having a question flung at them when it is not obvious whether they are intended to answer it or not. If you are asking a rhetorical question, make it obvious that you do not require an answer! This is a lesson I learnt to my cost when preaching in a borstal – where the answers received were nothing like the ones I was hoping for! You should not use questions, either, as an excuse for not doing your homework. While some of scripture is a mystery, some of it is not if we work at it hard enough. The preacher who skates over a passage and then asks the congregation whether they know what it means is shirking his or her duty. Don't be fooled into thinking that the odd pertinent question will give you the powerful edge it requires if you haven't tried by all other means to create it. Be cautious, too, about the staccato effect produced by heaping questions on top of each other in rapid succession. To the listener, this can feel very aggressive, and may cause them to retreat from the preaching and withdraw their interest.

Silence

Silence is a vastly underrated asset in preaching. The power of a silent pause to allow the previous point to soak in, or to pave the way for the next one, should not be underestimated. Think of that silent moment like the space on a white page which allows the text to shine out. Think of it like the vast empty spaces in a huge cathedral which allow you to appreciate the statues and the stained-glass windows all the more. It is a real test of the preacher's nerve to use silence properly. Time will pass much slower for you as speaker during a pause than it will for the congregation. I once started a sermon with a whole, timed minute's silence in order to emphasise how much we want God to speak to us. From where I was standing, it felt like at least an hour! You may also be afraid that people will think that your silence is accidental because you have lost your place or your nerve. If you use it well, they will soon realise that this is not the case. As with the questions, make sure you don't use it too often, or it will lose its impact.

Voice modulation

Charles Hadden Spurgeon was a great nineteenth-century preacher. Some people claim that his voice was so captivating that, if he had possessed a phone book, he could have read it out and still made it interesting. Sadly, the voice of some preachers is so monotone and boring that they can make the most passionate scripture passage sound like the phone book! Your voice is an instrument that God has asked you to play on his behalf – so play it for all you are worth. Play it loud, hitting the top notes and making the rafters rattle. Play it soft and have everyone straining on the edge of their seats to catch the next syllable. We should not allow politicians to corner the market on passionate speech. Listen to a recording of your last sermon. Is it all delivered in the same tone, or does your voice rise and fall, giving light and shade to the pictures you are painting? If variety is lacking, then you can learn to introduce it. While we all have a natural inclination in speech pattern and voice modulation, this behaviour can be unlearned. Like a right-handed stroke patient learning to write with their left hand, we can teach ourselves to speak differently if it serves a higher purpose. Try each time you preach to consciously introduce different tones, and monitor the recordings to see how successful you have been. It is worth remembering, too, that our natural inclination whenever we speak in public is to speak too quickly. If you speak too slowly in your own hearing, it will probably sound all right to everyone else.

Facial expression

One of the reasons we love to talk about important things face to face is because we read as much from facial expressions as we do from the words themselves. This is why international corporations invest thousands of pounds in video-conferencing facilities. It is also what gave rise to third-generation mobile phones. Is your face enlivened by your preaching? Has your enthusiasm for your subject invaded every sinew and muscle of your body, including your face? Often, our nerves and tension when we are new to public speaking mean that we tend to fix our face in a single expression – either a severe and earnest frown or a kind of rictus smile. If your trusted friend tells you that this is happening, you need to take steps before you begin to speak. Find yourself a quiet corner before the service begins where no-one will see you. Pronounce the sound 'eee', pushing the corners of your mouth as far as they will go to one side and the other. Alternate this with the sound 'aw', extending your mouth to top and bottom as far as it will go. Once you have repeated this exercise a few times, your face muscles will relax. It's probably best not to do it in the pulpit, though!

Of course, as Christian communicators, we have something on our side the likes of which men like Aristotle could not dream of – God's Holy Spirit. Every Sunday, he performs a miracle where our ordinary words are turned into heavenly communication. Scholars like to speculate about whether the miracle at Pentecost, when God's Word was proclaimed in many languages, was a miracle of hearing on the part of the crowd or speaking on the part of the apostles. Perhaps it was both – but, whichever it was, the miracle was wrought by God's Holy Spirit. As with all Christian service, preaching is a marriage of his blessing and our effort. We should plunder the resources of rhetoric and use every trick in the communicator's book as if we did not have the Spirit's help, while all the time rejoicing in the fact that we do.

S is for structured

Why not Spirit-led or Strong, or even Spontaneous, you might ask? Of course, we have already spoken about being Spirit-led in our chapter on pneumatic preaching, and we hope all that has been said so far will lead to strong preaching. Many, however, would see structure as the enemy of strong preaching. They would consider it as the resort of the weak and less spiritually minded preacher. This is not the case.

As with many disciplines, the novice preacher often rushes to throw off the shackles of structure too soon. Breaking the rules before you have learnt them can lead to disappointing results. When I first started to learn photography, my father encouraged me to write down the details of every single photograph as it was taken – aperture, exposure setting and so on. At the time it was a real nuisance, but it taught me the rudiments of photography as an art form, so that I can now bend it to my advantage. Many a new preacher feels that structure is an unnecessary straitjacket, and discards it in the name of freedom. They end up like the father of the bride at a wedding reception I once attended. At the last minute, he discarded his notes, saying that he 'didn't need them' – and then spent the next twenty minutes proving that in fact he did! Communicators of all kinds, whether playwrights, politicians, generals or poets, have proved over the course of thousands of years that structure is a necessary part of oral communication. Writing to his ordination candidates in 1859, Bishop Samuel Wilberforce advised them thus: 'Let every sermon be one subject, well divided and thoroughly worked out; and let all tend to this highest purpose, simply to exalt before your people Christ crucified (cited in the College of Preachers' *Journal*, July 2001, p. 103; used by permission of the College of Preachers).

Of course, it is no *simple* matter to exalt Christ crucified; but structure and focus can help us a long way towards doing it. Although we might regard Wilberforce's advice as unduly restrictive, it is often those sermons which have two or three or more foci which end up having no focus at all! That said, there are a number of different ways in which our material can be structured.

Hidden structure

Where there is a hidden structure, this may be apparent to the preacher but not to the listeners. Often, such a structure may be dictated by the passage itself. Thus, a sermon on a parable, for instance, may be structured thus:

1. Why and when the parable was told
2. The parable itself
3. Christ's private explanation of the parable to the disciples.

The congregation will not be aware of the divisions within the structure; but the preacher appears to move seamlessly through the parable from beginning to end. The preacher, on the other hand, is kept from meandering by this rough guideline.

A sermon on the opening chapter of an epistle may have a similar hidden structure:

1. who wrote it
2. who received it

3. how they were greeted
4. what they will be told.

Once again, the congregation will not be made aware of the internal divisions within the sermon. Instead, they are eased into the epistle and introduced to the key issues in a logical way. The preacher, though, has a road map for the sermon drawn from commentary-based research. The structure outlined above guards against assuming too much prior knowledge on the one hand, and delving too much into the overall themes of the letter on the other. It acts as a guide and a check for the preacher.

A thematic sermon may also use the hidden-structure approach. A sermon on a theme inspired by the news headlines, such as poverty or slavery, might run like this:

1. a description of the contemporary issue
2. evidence that this is a broad theme within the Bible
3. application of a specific biblical story to a specific contemporary example.

Using this approach prevents the preacher from meandering between the contemporary and biblical worlds in a way which might lose the listener on the journey.

Exostructure

Today, it is easier than ever to make the structure of the sermon accessible to those who hear it. Presentation software such as PowerPoint, and affordable data projectors, mean that many preachers can set out the structure of their sermon for all to see. For visual learners in the congregation, this can be a great help. Each point can be summarised in a few words on the screen, and eventually all can be displayed together in order to summarise the sermon's message. It is important, however, to exercise restraint in the use of this technology. For a thorough examination of the use of this technology, take a look at Jackie Sheppard's little book *Beyond the OHP*. However, there are two particular concerns to mention here. The first is that light letters on a dark background are easier to read. The second is that any wording should be restricted to simple bullet points. Furthermore, the sermon should not be so reliant on technology that it cannot function without it. A structure represented in a PowerPoint presentation should be so embedded within the sermon that the preaching can continue without it if necessary. As a person who relies heavily on visual support for my sermon structures, I was taught a costly lesson when preaching in India, where electricity was at best sporadic! A sermon with a clear structure, whether displayed in a graphic way or not, will be of particular help to the analytical learners in the congregation. People who like to organise their thoughts in an ordered way will appreciate this approach.

1 ... 2 ... 3 ... a ... b ... c

Whether you are displaying your points on a high-tech data projector, an old-fashioned OHP or even a blackboard, don't be afraid of simplicity. Although the three-point sermon in general and the three-point alliterated sermon in particular have become the butt of many jokes, that is not a reason to discard them altogether. Any device which helps people to retain what they have heard and learnt deserves serious consideration. I can still remember a sermon I heard on prayer at least thirty years ago because of its clear and obvious structure. The main thing is that the structure should be the servant of the sermon and not the other way round. Don't, whatever you do, shape your biblical material purely to fit in with some neat structure you already have in your head. Preachers should not treat their biblical theme as Procrustes of old treated his guests – stretching them to fit his bed if they were too short, and lopping bits off if they were too long. If people remember your three points *solely* because they began with the same letter, then it is a fair bet that the sermon has failed to hit its mark. If, on the other hand, they can remember two points and after some head-scratching remember the third because it began with the same letter, then your creativity has served you and your congregation well.

T is for teamwork

When I was ordained in 1992, the order of service carried the following message on it:

> To every baby-sitter, cake-baker, prayer-supporter, morale-booster, car-mender, shoulder-to-cry-on-profferer, financial backer, and helper of every sort who has made this ordination, indeed this ministry, possible, thanks.

It was not just a clever way of saying 'thank you', but contained a real seam of theological truth. Right at the core of our understanding of Church and Kingdom is the belief that all ministry is team ministry. This applies to the preacher in the pulpit, the evangelist in the tent and the missionary in the school just as much as it does to the member of the prayer or the music team. God so ordains things that we need each other. The 'geography' of preaching tends to undermine this, since one person stands out at the front and everyone else listens. It is easy for the casual observer, or even for the preacher, to think that the preacher is doing it all alone. This is not so.

God

When Moses was first commissioned by God to speak up for him in Pharaoh's court and beyond, he all but refused, pleading that he was not, and never had been, gifted as a speaker. God, however, reminded him that even the power of speech itself was a divine gift: 'Who gave man his mouth? Who makes him deaf or mute? Who gives him sight or makes him blind? Is it not I, the Lord?' (Exodus 4:11).

Every preacher needs to remember this. Even the act of speech itself is a collaborative one with God. We do not speak *for* God, as if he were mute and required us in order to express his thoughts. Much less do we speak *as* God, as if we could understand his thoughts with such clarity that we could pass them on untainted. Rather, we speak *with* him. His perfection is revealed through our imperfection. His clarity shines through our muddle. Preaching is 'truth through personality', even where that personality is flawed. Often, a preacher can feel like a champion striding out to do battle when he or she heads for the pulpit. The pulpit can seem like a lonely place as we seek to speak up for God from it. However, even while preaching, we are engaged in teamwork with God. We do our 'bit' as we speak the words we have been given, and he does his 'bit' as they are applied to the lives of those who listen. There is a kind of alchemy to preaching, whereby the plain rocks of our human vocabulary are turned to gold. God is the alchemist.

Congregation

It is often said that the congregation 'gets the preacher it deserves'. This is undoubtedly true, because preaching is intended to be a co-operative venture, and where there is no co-operation there is little blessing. This teamwork begins when the preacher is first entrusted with the task of preaching, on either a one-off or an ongoing basis. In entrusting him or her with the task, the congregation places a lot of trust in the preacher, but it also agrees to pray for the preacher through the preaching process. If we want to be fed on a Sunday, we need to be praying for the person doing the feeding all through the week. While a good prayer meeting immediately before a service gives a tremendous boost to the preacher, the same kind of concerted prayer should be going up all through the week while the sermon is being written. There is an element of teamwork, too, while the preacher is actually preaching the sermon. Enthusiastic and attentive listening can make all the difference to the sermon's effectiveness. There is a qualitative difference between a kind of listening which is merely resentful tolerance, and a listening which has the listeners on the edge of their seats hungrily waiting for the next word. In certain traditions, this is acknowledged by both preacher and people. In some black majority churches, the preacher will call for an 'amen' from the people to be sure that they have understood his point, while the congregation may call out 'Help him, Lord!' if they feel the preacher is struggling.

The teamwork continues after the sermon is over, too. Many preachers cry out for some kind of feedback beyond the limp handshake and the 'thank you, preacher' which is the norm at the church door. Where preaching is acknowledged as teamwork, the preacher will encourage and absorb feedback from the congregation in order to ensure that the preaching 'hits the spot'. This is not to say that people will necessarily enjoy the preaching – few, for example, would have 'enjoyed' the preaching of a Jeremiah or an Ezekiel. It is rather to suggest that they are absorbing it and letting the preacher know whether it is too esoteric or too earthly, too simple or too complex. In this way, preacher and people work together to ensure that preaching 'works'.

Church leadership

Good preaching is very costly in terms of preparation time. A good sermon, just like a masterpiece of creative art, cannot be produced in a short time. For many preachers, their only opportunity to reach their entire congregation at once is the Sunday-morning service, which means the sermon is absolutely critical. If that sermon is to be effective, it will require a considerable investment of time. When Dr Billy Graham first started preaching, he estimated that every fifteen minutes in the pulpit required at least two hours in the study. Personally, I would find that to be a conservative estimate, especially when one is new to the task. Although many in churches may acknowledge this need for time investment, they fail to recognise its impact on other areas of church life. Time spent on sermon preparation is time that cannot be spent on other elements of church life, be it visiting the sick or poring over budgets or strategy papers. This allocation of time must be negotiated with the church leadership wherever possible, in order to ensure that there is no unnecessary resentment and that preacher and church can work together. If the church wants a preacher who can deliver a quality product on a Sunday, they must allow time for that product to be crafted. In this, the church leadership must lead the way. Furthermore, any decisions on the allocation of the minister's time must be clearly communicated to the congregation.

Although, of necessity, preaching is an act that can only be performed by one person at a time, the pulpit is no place for prima donnas. Preachers must be keenly aware that their preaching relies on the grace of God and the support of the congregation. The apostle Paul, whose preaching changed the course of history, and who preached before crowds, kings and emperors, freely acknowledged his dependence on others. Speaking about his preaching mission, he urged the Corinthians to pray for him:

On him we have set our hope that he will continue to deliver us, as you help us by your prayers. Then many will give thanks on our behalf for the gracious favour granted us in answer to the prayers of many.

(2 Corinthians 1:10–11)

In these two verses, although he will go on to underline his status and authority as an apostle, he models the interdependence which should be a hallmark of the preaching ministry.

U is for unfinished

When we first start out in preaching, one of the pitfalls into which we all fall is the temptation to preach every sermon we have ever thought of all in one. This may include any or all of the following:

- the hell-fire sermon
- the get-saved-quick sermon
- the 'problem-with-the-church-today' sermon
- the 'God-loves-you-anyway' sermon
- the 'carry-on-regardless' sermon
- the 'urgent-call-to-mission' sermon
- the 'pray-or-perish' sermon.

Not surprisingly, a sermon which combines all of these will not only be exhausting to preach but also very exhausting to hear! As is often the case, a multiple focus rapidly becomes no focus at all. Furthermore, as the foci get multiplied, so does the length. A prolonged sermon can be like a diluted pot of old tea – increasingly lacking in flavour and ever more insipid. As hard as it might be, especially when we are unsure how many preaching opportunities will be given to us, we need to accept that we cannot say everything we would like to say. This is made slightly easier if we recognise that in one sense every sermon is unfinished ...

Monday-to-Friday church

Years ago, I attended a new ministers' retreat and was asked to write on a large piece of paper where my church was to be found at 11 o'clock on a Monday morning. Not surprisingly, I was not expected to say that the church *building* was to be found in exactly the same place as it was on a Sunday! Instead, I wrote words like 'school', 'work', 'park' and 'office'. Once your sermon is over and the church empties out into the streets and on into people's houses, the real work of your words begins. This may start with the long-established tradition of 'having the preacher for lunch' as your sermon is dissected over the lunch table. More importantly, though, it may continue around the water-cooler or on the bus. If you didn't say everything you wanted to, you should not worry. The Word of God will develop a life of its own in these subsequent conversations which you could not possibly have imagined, and over which you have no control.

Acted, not annunciated

The real worth of a sermon is to be measured not by the words that you said (or omitted) but by their impact on people's lives. The most eloquent sermon in the world which leaves people impressed but unchanged has very little value. Conversely, the simplest and barest sermon in the world which changes people's lives is a cause for rejoicing in heaven and earth. Over the years, I have researched the relationship between preaching and translation. I have been fascinated by the way in which a preacher, like a translator, has to move between two linguistic worlds – in this case, the world of the Bible and the world inhabited by the congregation. As he or she makes the journey between the two, all kinds of decisions must be made about how things are phrased in order to get as much meaning as possible across. First of all, the translator must pass the original (or source) text through a series of linguistic filters in order to understand it properly, rather like a preacher using Bible commentaries. The new (or target) text will then be read by many others in order to establish its effectiveness in the target language. Along the way, some meaning is added and some is lost. Translation is a very complex science, and many books have been devoted to it. However, the final test of a translation's worth is not linguistic or scientific analysis, but whether or not people understand it. If I translate a road sign which says 'turn left for the station', and every car drives straight on past because the words are not understood, the translation has failed. In a similar vein, your sermon will never be finished until people start applying it. A frustrating aspect of this is that the fulfilment may happen at a time and place which you are unable to see.

A relay marathon

Although the relay marathon is not an Olympic event, it should be familiar to all those who read their Bibles. So often in scripture, we see that the purposes of God are achieved over time, with the baton handed from one key figure to another as it passes. Thus Moses passes the baton onto Joshua without living to see the Promised Land; David passes the baton onto Solomon without living to see the temple built, and so on. Many of us are unlikely to see all the fruit we long to see in one ministry, let alone one sermon. Instead, we must develop a kind of biblical patience which recognises that our preaching ministry will always be unfinished. This need not be such a bad thing. Schubert's hauntingly beautiful 'Unfinished Symphony', with only two of its three movements written, has probably had as much impact as many of his completed works. We must be patient over the long term when we look for results from preaching. Interestingly, the New Testament word for 'patience' is *makrothumia*, which means 'long-mindedness'. With that long-minded perspective, it is easier to accept that some things are best left to preach another day.

Most people who read this book will have seen the bumper sticker which calls for God to give us patience 'and hurry'! However, I find the following story more helpful. A tourist reputedly stopped on his way round an Oxford college to admire the perfect emerald lawn which graced the college's quadrangle. Thinking of his bumpy, brown, uneven lawn back home, he stopped the groundsman and asked: 'Say, how do I get my lawn to look like that?' The old man paused, leaning on the handle of his lawnmower, and took his time as he removed his cap. Looking the tourist in the eye, he answered with his deep Oxfordshire burr: 'Well, sir, you cuts it and rolls it carefully for 400 years, and it just comes like that'!

If your preaching is unfinished when the sermon is over, there is no need to worry. There will be other sermons, and indeed other preachers to come after you – and God has all the time in the world!

V is for vulnerable

This is probably a terrible confession to make, but not only am I an advertisements junkie, my favourite advert is for lager! It features a row of ducks being shot down mercilessly at a fairground arcade. After glugging the requisite drink, they then return equipped with tanks to exact their revenge on the marksmen! It appeals to me because so many preachers feel just like that – sitting ducks ready to be shot down by their congregations. Preacher are vulnerable – which is one of the reasons James warns us that no-one should rush into preaching: 'Not many of you should presume to be teachers, my brothers, because you know that we who teach will be judged more strictly' (James 3:1).

Notice, though, that James says 'not many' rather than 'not any'. The fear of scrutiny and judgement should not put us off preaching entirely. In fact, our vulnerability as preachers can have both negative and positive consequences.

Negative aspects

The devil

The devil can and does attack preachers simply because God makes use of them. A preacher disabled by lack of confidence or doubt about his or her own ability strikes a crippling blow at the heart of the Church. For the devil to target preachers is not unlike the military tactic of bringing down the standard-bearer or the bugler on the battlefield. With these men down, the troops will neither rally nor heed their orders. Preachers are prime targets for the devil's attack.

Shakespeare syndrome

I love acting, and did a great deal of it at both school and university. However, my worst acting experience ever was Shakespeare's *Richard II*. It wasn't because of the script – which is wonderful. Nor was it because of the setting – a ruined abbey on the banks of the River Thames. In fact, it was because of the Shakespeare enthusiasts in the audience with the script open on their laps, following every single word with their fingers – something they would not do with any other playwright. Years later, I am sometimes reminded of them as I look at a congregation – Bibles open on laps and scrutinising every word.

Continuity department

Every once in a while, there will be a programme on television based entirely around viewers' opinions of other programmes which have been screened. As well as the usual complaints about language and repeats, there will be a batch of letters from eagle-eyed continuity experts, spotting that the colour of a dress or the position of a plant pot has changed from one scene to the next. These people live in churches too. They will hold you to account for something you said two weeks or even two years ago, if you later appear to contradict or challenge it.

Goldfish bowl

Most preachers live cheek by jowl with those to whom they preach. They meet them at the shops, they park their cars next to them, they drink coffee with them and they worship alongside them. This means that all those preachers must live with the consequences of their preaching. If, for instance, they preach on the need to 'go green' and avoid using the car for unnecessary journeys, they can be almost certain that someone will spot them when they drive the quarter of a mile to the church! If they preach about buying fairly traded goods on a Sunday, they should not be surprised if a passing church member scrutinises the contents of their shopping basket on a Monday.

Positive aspects

Accountability

In fact, the example we have just used brings me to one of the most positive aspects of vulnerability. Trying though it is, preachers should live up to the words they have preached. A preacher who preaches fair trade and then shops irresponsibly, for instance, should be brought to account. Furthermore, it is good that people are scrutinising their Bibles to check that the preacher is doing justice to the scriptures. Remember, this is what the Christians in Berea were commended for: 'Now the Bereans were of more noble character than the Thessalonians, for they received the message with great eagerness and examined the scriptures every day to see if what Paul said was true' (Acts 17:12).

Years ago, some churches used to have Berean Guilds in their Sunday schools, where eager young boys and girls were encouraged to study their Bibles until they knew them backwards.

Perhaps those boys and girls are now some of the adults in our congregations who follow the preacher with an index finger on the page of their Bible!

When it comes to continuity, perhaps preachers should be flattered that anyone even remembers what they said in sermons gone by! Maybe, like Jesus, there are good reasons for saying things that apparently contradict each other – just as he did with saying on one occasion that 'he who is not with me is against me' (Matthew 12:30) and on another that 'whoever is not against you is for you' (Luke 9:30). There are times when a preacher may have moved on in his or her understanding, and the challenge from a careful listener can give the opportunity to explain why.

Thin-skinned

Don't let anyone ever tell you that a preacher should be thick-skinned. If your skin is too thick, you will not be able to feel the jolts, knocks and bruises which your congregation feels. Even though it is a mixed blessing to be vulnerable to people, it is still a blessing. Consider the life of Jeremiah, surely the figure among the major prophets most similar to Christ, who would follow on. At times, he is almost crushed by the insult and opprobrium of others, and yet it allows him to speak words whose edge can still be felt centuries later. The word 'almost' is significant, though. Like a great actor portraying emotion so intense the audience can feel it, but not so caught up that he cannot play the next scene, the preacher also needs to 'keep a little back' for the rest of the sermon – and for whatever ministry follows immediately after it.

Open-souled

This is not a reference to the kind of footwear the preacher should sport – although socks and sandals may not be the best! In fact, it is another reference to the prophets of old. The secret of their power as prophets lay not only in their vulnerability to people, but also in their vulnerability to God. The hearts which were so readily pierced by the suffering of their countrymen bore wounds of God's finger too. Think, for instance, of Hosea, whose passionate poetry was the product of his passionate and costly encounter with the living God.

Warning

As we have seen, vulnerability has its positive and its negative aspects. However, a preacher should never use emotional vulnerability in a way which is dishonest. Displaying your own emotions when preaching, so long as you are not rendered incapable, can certainly have its place. However, displaying your emotions in order to achieve a particular effect on your listeners smacks of cynical manipulation, and is to be avoided. Being vulnerable is one thing, but being dishonest is another.

W is for wholehearted

Faced with a group of enthusiastic but naïve disciples, Jesus warned them that the road ahead would be a difficult one. Not only this, but he went further and said that half-hearted disciples were an unacceptable liability for the Kingdom: 'No-one who puts his hand to the plough and then looks back is fit for service in the Kingdom of God' (Luke 9:62).

In similar vein, those who enter on the ministry of preaching and do it half-heartedly are not suited to the task. Preaching is such a high calling, with such high stakes, that it must be done in a wholehearted way or not at all. Apathetic preaching breeds apathetic listening, which in turn leads to apathetic discipleship. Such preaching is, surely, not worthy of the name? After all that we have said about preaching providing a space to encounter God and a means of transformation, we cannot expect it to work in anything but the most wholehearted way. Wholehearted preaching demands so much of us that it is not a cerebral or a physical or a spiritual thing, but all three.

Body

Although we have noted in the chapter on kinetic preaching that physical movement should be avoided if it is excessive or distracting, it nonetheless has its place. If it allows you to be yourself, or to underline the points which you are making, then it can be a real help. However, even without bold and expressive gestures, preaching is a demanding physical act. Communicating in public under the undivided attention of a congregation is physically draining. This physical fatigue is felt not only in the voice but also in the whole body, and will probably be entirely disproportionate to the amount of time you have spent on your feet. While I would not advocate the construction of specialist preachers' gyms, and certainly would not presume to tell you what kind of exercise to take, it is incumbent upon the preacher to take good care of his or her body. Our lungs, our hands, our feet and our voices are as much tools of our trade as a weightlifter's biceps or a concert pianist's fingers, and we need to take good care of them. A reasonable degree of physical fitness should be seen as a requirement of the job for the preacher. As a preacher, our physical body is a precious instrument which God has given to us in order to fulfil our high calling. As such a treasured charge, it has to be looked after.

Mind

If you are just starting out as a preacher, resolve in your mind right now that you will never use the phrase 'that will do' concerning a sermon. If you have been preaching for a long time, ask God for the strength never to use it again. A foolhardy student once reputedly told Charles Spurgeon, the great preacher, that he had run out of time for sermon preparation, so he had *just* done a 'simple gospel message'. The great man was incandescent at the student's attitude – both that he should have allowed himself to run out of time, and that he had dismissed gospel preaching as a *simple* alternative. No preaching is simple, least of all gospel preaching! We all have different mental capacities; but, whatever the capacity might be, the expectation is that we will use it all up, like the widow's mite.

Are you researching your Bible passage as hard as *you* can? Have you thought as hard as *you* can about how to express its particular truths? Like any other discipline, we must train our minds to do this. Furthermore, when we find them slipping out of the habit, we must coax and cajole and push them back into it. Sometimes, the demands of balancing preaching with other duties mean that we cut down on this mental labour. While it is possible to disguise a lack of mental preparation in the short term, it will soon begin to show. A sermon with cut corners will have no corners left with which to prod the conscience! As with our physical fitness, we must seek to retain our mental fitness and agility too. This means that we must keep reading – from both sacred and secular sources. If research is to be believed, we should complete the odd crossword too!

Soul

The meanings of the biblical words for 'soul' are notoriously hard to pin down. The word most often used in the New Testament is 'psyche', which can also mean 'life'. It refers to the unknowable, indescribable yet obviously present inner life, which distinguishes us. Perhaps we get closest to it when we describe a particular piece of music as 'having soul'. If we are to preach, then we must expect to throw not only body and mind, but our very souls into it too. It is almost impossible to preach without some degree of emotional involvement. Although this will vary according to our particular personality and character, we must invest something of ourselves in the sermon. As we saw in the previous chapter, Jeremiah gives a particularly good example of this. He was a preacher and a prophet with a particularly sensitive soul. This allowed him to empathise with the fate of his people in a particularly acute way, feeling their pain and describing it as if it were his own: 'Why is my pain unending and my wound grievous and incurable?' (Jeremiah 15:18).

His personal involvement had another side, though, causing him to suffer cruelly under the rejection and the jibes of his people. The two-edged sword of this sensitivity makes him the most poignant of the prophets. In Acts 20, we are privileged to see the apostle Paul bare his soul in a way that he does nowhere else. In a touching farewell to the elders of the church at Ephesus, he assures them that he has 'served the Lord with great humility and with tears', and furthermore that he had 'not hesitated to preach anything which would be helpful to you' (Acts 20:19–20). This is wholehearted preaching indeed.

A friend of mine with many years of preaching experience all around the world nonetheless found it an exceptionally demanding activity. Despite his ability to prepare sermons with apparently effortless ease, and to preach 'off the cuff' when called upon to do so, he did not find it easy. Often at the end of a busy Sunday, we would compare notes, and he would say that after preaching he felt as if he had experienced '10,000 volts passed through me'. The parallel works on many levels. For a start, there is the fact that a conductor passes electricity from its power source to the place where it is needed. Secondly, it is the end product rather than the conductor which people remember. Thirdly, and most appropriately for us here, it is a dangerous and risky thing to find oneself the conduit for such powerful energy! Wholehearted preaching is a dangerous, wonderful and exhausting experience – but that really is the only way to do it.

X is for *x*

We are almost at the end of our alphabetical journey through preaching, and therefore this might seem a particularly odd thing to say at this juncture. However, it is quite possible to take too much notice of preaching. By that I do not, of course, mean that it is not important. I mean, instead, that it is not the only thing which matters. When we exalt the role of preaching too much, worship becomes merely an adjunct to the preaching, a kind of warm-up to the main event. Clearly, this will not do. Nor should we participate in the cult of the preacher, which perpetuates the myth that the preacher is the one truly important person in church, and that the rest of us merely dance attendance on him or her. Undoubtedly the preacher's role is vital, as we have seen in the previous twenty-three chapters. The preacher acts as a conduit for the Word of God, allowing it to be experienced and participating in the re-creative work of the Spirit of God. This is a high calling indeed. It must be set alongside other high callings, though. It takes its place alongside other gifts and ministries, such as the leading of worship, the writing and playing of truly inspirational music, and costly intercessory prayer. For many of us, preaching could not proceed without the practical gifts of those who put out seats for the congregation to sit on, others who control the sound system so they can hear, and so on. The place of preaching is special, though not unique. So, what makes a preacher? What are the 'X factors' for which you should look in yourself and others?

The humble showman

You will not be surprised to see the word 'humble' here. There is no room in the pulpit for a big ego. If we preach because we think we know better than everyone else, or if we preach because we love the sound of our own voice, then preaching is not the role for us. If we preach because we thrive on other people's undivided attention, and allow ourselves to believe that every word we say is profound and worthy, we will soon stumble in our preaching ministry. There must be a humble acceptance of God's anointing, and a humble desire to serve those who entrust us with their attention. However, there is also an element of showmanship in preaching. By that I do not mean a self-seeking bent or any insincerity in our presentation. Rather, it is a comfort with the limelight and an acceptance that our true place is in the public eye. A showman is someone who desires to do the best for his or her audience, and is willing to make personal sacrifices in order to achieve it. A showman is someone who understands that the dynamics of public communication are entirely different to those of private conversation. He or she realises that at times it will take big gestures and strong words to engage the attention of the audience when neither would be necessary in one-to-one conversation. A showman is someone who knows that the 'show must go on' and who will do all within his or her power to ensure that it does. Could you be such a showman?

The wise fool

The figure of the fool has a rich and illustrious history. Across the centuries, and in different cultures, the fool has been the butt of jokes and even cruelty, but he is also seen to be the one who speaks the uncomfortable truth. Consider the Shakespearean fool in the court of King Lear, for instance. Though often cruelly struck and abused by his master, he is the only one who really understands the king's undignified descent into madness. A preacher in this mould is someone who is willing to speak the awkward truths which people fear but avoid. Such preachers will risk opprobrium and worse, provided it means they can be true to their calling and their message. Could you be such a person? This is a particular challenge when you preach regularly in the context of a particular congregation. Could you point out the besetting sin of a church even if they pay your wages? Even when you travel from place to place as a preacher, you may need to be willing to wear the fool's hat and bear the fool's kind of unpopularity. Could you be the lone voice to critique an element of popular culture even when everybody else regards it as innocuous? If you can, you stand in a long line of preachers stretching all the way from Jeremiah in the Old Testament, to Jesus and Peter in the New, and on into preaching heroes of the modern age such as Martin Luther King. As somebody once said to me, 'rather a fool for Christ than anybody else's fool'.

The woolly shepherd

Obviously, I am not advocating a woolly approach to preaching, where sermons are vague, unfocused and meandering. In truth, I am still haunted by the occasion years ago when I asked a senior colleague to let me know what he thought of a particular sermon, and he left a cartoon of a woolly sheep on my desk! The description of the preacher as a woolly shepherd is to do with the attitude of the preacher rather than the content of his or her sermons. Though your preaching places you in a position of responsibility and even authority among your fellow Christians, never forget that you wear the same clothing as they do. You are dressed in wool just like they are – for we are all among the lost sheep found by the Good Shepherd. You may be in a unique position to guide and coax and encourage the sheep along their way – but you are still one of them. The longer we go on preaching, and the more accustomed we become to the sound of our own voice over against the silence of others, the more we can become convinced of our special status. It is for this reason that every preacher, even the most concise and incisive one in the world, needs to be woolly too!

Following the stupendous success of *The X Factor* talent-show format, the franchise has now been sold to countries around the world. Audiences in their millions tune in to watch singers do their best to prove that they have 'the X factor'. The interesting thing is that it is never defined. Young singers are simply told that they either have it or they don't. Thankfully, the world of preaching has never caught the X-factor bug, with preachers vying with each other to garner votes and win the prize. However, it is worth remembering that, for us, X is the first letter of Christ in the New Testament. For us, a truly successful preacher is one who carries the hallmark of his or her Lord in his or her preaching ministry. Simple, Godly inspired and powerful words show that he or she has the real X factor.

Y is for you

Some days, you will feel like preaching is the most natural thing in the world to you. As you open your mouth to speak, you will feel like a bird spreading its wings to take to the skies. Your heart will beat faster, your spirits will lift and you will find yourself borne along with the excitement of it all. Other days, it will be a quite different story. Far from feeling that you are giving voice to God's Word, you will feel that you are personally responsible for preventing others from hearing it. You will feel awkward and diffident, and it will seem as if all your phrases come out the wrong way. Whenever that happens, you need to remember one very important thing. This is the fact that God chose you. He did this with a full awareness of your past foibles and your future failings. God chose you, and he does not make mistakes – ever.

On the day that I was ordained to Christian ministry, one of my college lecturers preached at the service. He chose to preach on the story of Gideon – the youngest and weakest member of the smallest family of the least significant clan of a smaller tribe of Israel. In particular, he picked out the text in Judges 6:34, where the young man Gideon picks up the trumpet and blows it with all his might. The verse describes it in a particularly arresting way: 'The spirit of the Lord clothed himself with Gideon and he blew upon the trumpet'.

I have carried that image with me, through good sermons and bad. God has chosen to give voice to his Word through me, even knowing me as he does. I may be the trumpet – but his is the breath! There are numerous aspects to this.

Your personality

Are you a hothead or a cool character? Are you phlegmatic or passionate? Remember that the God who chose you to preach also chose people as different as Jonah on the one hand and Peter on the other. God chose you with full knowledge of your personality, and with the specific intention that it should come out in your preaching. When we try to deny our personality in the pulpit, we end up sounding very artificial, like great music played on a cheap and tinny loudspeaker. Not only that, but also people who recognise that your personae in and out of the pulpit are radically different will soon decide to avoid one or other or both of them! In the end, this is a matter of trust: do we trust God's judgement in choosing a person like us to be a preacher? Of course, this does not mean that we give vent to the less Christian aspects of our character, such as a jealousy of others and their gifts, or an inclination to be judgemental. Instead, we yield our character, such as it is, to God, and trust him to mould it even as we serve him in preaching.

Your experience

I have many old books in my study bought in various second-hand bookshops over the years. One of the most interesting is an edition of Thomas à Kempis' *Imitation of Christ*, printed in the late eighteenth century. It has a leather binding with fine toolwork down the edges of the cover and beautiful woodcuts inside. However, it is the shape of the cover which makes it interesting. If you hold the book in your hand, you can tell that it has been held that way, in that position, hundreds or maybe thousands of times. Look carefully, and you can see that the leather is worn down where it has been grasped firmly over the years. Far from being pristine, this book has been used and worn down through use. Its scars make it interesting. Believe it or not, it is the same with you. As you seek to imitate Christ in word and deed, it is the scars which make you interesting. Your experiences, even the negative ones, are the things which have shaped you into a tool for communication that God can use.

Your strengths

You have a number of strengths which may equip you to be a preacher. Perhaps you are an avid reader, which allows you to process comment on both the world and the Bible with great ease. Perhaps you are a keen observer of human life, which allows you to understand the people to whom you are preaching. You may also have other strengths, such as a ready sense of humour, good physical stamina or a mellifluous voice. Any and all of these can be used by the God who called you into this ministry. Don't disregard, either, other strengths whose application to preaching is less obvious. You might be surprised at the number and variety of strengths which can be put to good use in the pulpit. Read the biblical accounts of Paul's and Peter's preaching respectively. Paul's sermons are laced with his learning and his Jewish background, while Peter's ring with the passion which earned him praise and trouble in equal measure!

Your weaknesses

You might also be surprised to learn the weaknesses which beset some of the world's great preachers. Some of them are obvious physical problems, such as Christmas Evans' one eye or Jonathan Edwards' short sight. Martin Luther's weakness – a depression to which he referred as the 'black dog' – was less obvious. Charles Spurgeon, the great nineteenth-century preacher, was plagued by chronic self-doubt, and would occasionally have to be physically compelled into the pulpit by his deacons. That God should use such people should be a great encouragement to the rest of us when we feel our weakness. It may be that our weakness gives us a particular understanding of the needs of others. If we are especially anxious, we will understand the needs of those whose faith is gnawed away by worry. If we are inclined to look on the negative side of things, we will empathise with those who often find depression snapping at their heels. If our calling to preach makes us quake with fear, perhaps we will understand those who sit in church on a Sunday worrying about going into work on Monday.

There is another way in which our weaknesses can help us. They remind us of our humanity and keep us dependent on God in order to fulfil our ministry. Like Moses accepting his commission, like Jeremiah receiving the prophetic mantle, and like young Solomon acceding to the throne, we have to say to God: 'with your help or not at all'.

There is a television programme I occasionally watch where old cars are taken away into a garage and transformed beyond all recognition – or 'pimped'. Under layers of faux leather interiors, spinning wheel rims and unnecessary video screens, their old character gradually disappears. Be assured that this is not what God has chosen to do with you. He will, of course, continue to mould and change you, as he does with every Christian. However, it is you whom he has chosen, rather than someone else you might like to be. Right now, even today, he wants to use you as you are.

Z is for zeal

Do you ever want to 'answer back' when you are in church? Perhaps I am alone in suffering from this particular affliction. You see, whenever we say the Lord's Prayer together and we reach the line which says: 'forgive us as we forgive those who sin against us', a bit of me wants to stand up and shout: 'no, Lord, don't do it!' If God only forgives me as well as I forgive other people, I am probably in serious trouble! Another stimulus for my rebellious streak is the line in the old hymn which says: 'revive us, Lord, is zeal abating?' Why? Because I so want to shout out 'yes' – that's why. I look around me, and I see zeal most definitely abating, if not entirely abated! I see tired singers, tired musicians, tired parents, tired teenagers and even tired preachers. Perhaps you feel tired out by the prospect of preaching, whether you are facing your first or your 1,001st sermon.

Zeal-sappers

While preachers are undoubtedly a target for the devil, and while a tired preacher helps his evil cause no end, it is not helpful to lay all the blame at his door. There are a number of things which sap our zeal as preachers.

Fatigue

Many preachers come to the act of preaching from a week already ridiculously full. They have divided their time between young and old, strategy and sympathy, comfort and conflict to such an extent that there is little room left over for any kind of creative thought. The first thing is to acknowledge this. Don't beat yourself up supposing this to be a deep spiritual problem when it is only a physical one. Maybe, like Elijah after the clash on Mount Carmel, you're just exhausted and need a square meal and a long lie down! Although Elijah starts off by saying that he is so suicidal he wants to die – 'I have had enough, Lord, take my life, I am no better than my ancestors' (1 Kings 19:4–5) – it soon becomes apparent that exhaustion is a major factor. If you are suffering from this kind of chronic fatigue, the second thing is to acknowledge that this is not purely the preacher's problem. An unreasonable workload may be the result of overblown expectations on the church's and on the preacher's part. If your workload is exhausting you and the preaching is suffering as a result, you need to look at this very seriously with the church leadership. If the church wants a 'quality product' delivered on a Sunday, then the rest of your working life needs to make such a goal possible.

Criticism

We have said in our chapter on vulnerability that a preacher is a sensitive creature, and indeed must be. There are times when we need the person who will pull us up on our biblical accuracy or our cultural awareness. However, a constant barrage of criticism, or a single word sharpened to the point where it slips in between the leaves of the preacher's armour and pierces his or her heart, can do untold damage. If your zeal is altogether abated, look back over the past few weeks and try to remember what has been said to you. This is not in order to dwell unhelpfully on those destructive words, but rather to deal with them. To retain our armour image for a moment, it is all about finding where the arrowhead is buried in the soft tissue of the heart and pulling it out so that healing can begin.

Indifference

Some preachers would love to have feedback from their congregation, even if it were of the negative kind. Instead, there is ample evidence that they are met week by week with a kind of blank indifference. At first, this may seem preferable to any kind of negative feedback; but over time it erodes the preacher's zeal. 'Why bother,' one asks oneself, 'when they neither smile nor weep?' It is easy to feel that the words penetrate no further than the ears, let alone to the heart or mind. Met with this kind of indifference, the preacher's zeal is often the first casualty to fall.

Zeal-boosters

Rest

If you are too tired to preach, then the simple answer to your problem is to get some rest. Of course, you probably don't like to admit that you need it; but what is more important, your pride or God's Word? Apparently, the advice for the monks of St Benedict, if they caught one of their brothers dozing off during a sermon, was to leave him, on the grounds that if he were that tired he probably needed a sleep! Mike Graves draws attention to that story in his fabulous book *The Fully Alive Preacher*, where he describes the 'sacrament of napping' as 'a grand and glorious gift of God' (p. 55). Perhaps you should try it!

Food

When Elijah fell asleep after his long race from Mount Carmel and told the angel in no uncertain terms that he had had enough, he was twice woken up by God's messenger in order to eat some good food. For many preachers, spiritual hunger is an occupational hazard. They may find themselves in sole charge of a church, and the only sermons they ever hear are their own. If this is the case, they have to find other ways of receiving the food which the congregation takes for granted. As well as reading, and listening to Christian radio where available, they need to investigate the possibility of attending courses and conferences with a view to their spiritual well-being. Not only this, but the people they feed should expect to contribute towards the cost of such conferences, too. This is the principle Paul espouses in Galatians 6:6, when he says that 'anyone who receives instruction in the word must share all good things with his instructor'. I was once given a jar of marmalade by a grateful church member with this verse inscribed on the top. It was extremely welcome, although sometimes the gift may need to be of a more directly financial nature!

Variety

When zeal is flagging, a little variety can be a big help. This may be as simple as preparing your sermon on a Monday instead of a Friday, or as drastic as saying that you will only preach three out of every four sermons, and that others must be found to take your place. You could try preparing your sermon in a different context, too. How about taking up residence in a local coffee house or a local park while you mull over your notes? The stimulus of noise and different faces around you might be just what you need.

Loosen your grip

To say this at the end of these twenty-six chapters on preaching may seem like a very odd thing. However, it is possible to grasp onto preaching with an urgency that ends up undermining it. If you are a driver, imagine what would happen if you always grasped the steering wheel with such extreme urgency that your knuckles turned white! Preaching is an honour and a privilege; it is an urgent lifeline between God and his Church. None of this means, though, that you must cling onto it for dear life. Do your best, but accept that it will sometimes go better than at other times. Try your hardest, but acknowledge that God tries harder than any of us. Let him grip the pulpit, rather than you doing it – and perhaps, one day when you are not looking, your zeal will creep back in through the back door!

Before you preach

Now that you have made your way through the past twenty-six chapters, it is time to put knees to floor and pen to paper (or fingers to keyboard). In other words, it is time to preach. In the advice which follows, no prior knowledge or experience is assumed. If you have already been preaching for some time, you may find it helpful to revisit these basic techniques. Equally, you may find that they cause you to reflect on the practice you have honed over the years. If you are an experienced driver, have you ever travelled in the front seat alongside a new driver? As you note the careful position of their hands on the wheel, their meticulous mirror-checking and their observation skills, you have probably realised that many things have slipped since you passed your test! Perhaps this return to the basics will replenish what the years of experience have stolen or modified.

What you need

- A humble heart
- A quiet place
- Two pieces of paper and pen
- A Bible
- A generous allocation of time.

A humble heart

A preacher without a humble heart is a liability to both him- or herself and those who listen to him or her. Before we even begin to draft the sermon, let alone preach it, we need to fix the right attitude in our minds and hearts. We do not preach because we are interesting or special or captivating. We are not doing God and the people a favour by preaching. We preach because we are called, and other people listen because they believe us to be called. The first step in the preaching process is to peel away all the layers of self-importance and arrogance which may have attached themselves to us. Once that is done, we need to get on our knees, either metaphorically or physically (I would recommend the latter), and state again our complete and utter dependence upon the God who called us. If Eutychus is the patron saint of boring preachers (see Acts 20:9), then the patron verse for all preachers is John 15:5: 'Apart from me you can do nothing'.

If you are preparing to preach right now, then read that verse through again. Dwell on each word. Allow the Holy Spirit to drive each one into the soft tissue of your heart. A humble heart is worth more than all the theological degrees in the world when it comes to preaching.

A quiet place

As we have said in chapter 'Z', there may well be times in the future where you choose to vary the preaching experience by preparing your sermons in among the hustle and bustle of everyday life. You may choose to take up residence in a coffee shop, or even on a busy station platform. It is surprising how much freshness such a change of scene can bring to your preaching. However, that is all for later on. Right now, the important thing is to find a place where your mind is at peace and you stand a reasonable chance of being undisturbed. At this early stage of the preparation process, why not turn the computer off too? There will be time enough to use it later. The most important thing is to create a space and a time where God can penetrate your thoughts and your imagination with ease. Once you have found that quiet space on the outside, try to quieten things down on the inside too. List off your noisy thoughts. Tell God about all the things which are worrying you, the other jobs which are ganging up on you like angry bees trapped by a glass. Ask him to mind them, just for now, so that you can be quiet and think. The most important part of speaking, as a preacher, is listening.

Two pieces of paper and a pen

Of course, it could be a pencil, or wax crayon, or even a quill pen! The most important thing is that it is something you can 'scribble' with. At this early stage of preparing to preach, you do not want to over-organise your thoughts. You must be able to jot them down, score them out and draw lines between them or circles round them. The reasons for the two pieces of paper will become apparent in the next chapter, although suffice it to say here that one is for writing down what you think about the Bible passage, and the other is for writing down thoughts on how you might communicate it. These are two very different processes, as we shall see. There is also a good reason for placing these pieces of paper higher up the list than the Bible itself. Once you have humbled your heart and quietened your mind, you may well find that God has things to say to you about your congregation before you even open the Bible. Don't dismiss these, but scribble them down. Equally, he may draw your attention to the scrape of the tree branch on the window outside or the pattern of sunlight falling on the carpet. Remember Jeremiah, when he was just learning to be a prophet, albeit reluctantly. The first thing God showed him was an ordinary tree branch: 'The word of the Lord came to me: "What do you see, Jeremiah?" "I see a branch of an almond tree", I replied' (Jeremiah 1:11).

If there is any chance at all that such things might be significant, write them down. You can always score them out later if they don't seem so important in the cold light of day. As preachers, we are primarily servants of the Word, but we accept that God's resources for revelation are not restricted to the printed page.

A Bible

If you ever see a builder travelling on the train, you'll probably see a spirit-level sticking out of his toolbag. If you ever see a doctor (especially a newly qualified one), you will see a stethoscope round her neck. If you meet a surveyor, the chances are he will have a tape measure in his top pocket. These things are the tools of their trade, the badges of their office. For the preacher, the tool of the trade is a Bible. Old, new, bashed, pristine – whatever it looks like, the Bible is to the preacher what the spirit-level is to the builder or the tape measure to the surveyor. You simply cannot do without it. However, when it comes to the Bible you use as a preacher, there are some particular considerations.

Not too big

Although we may cherish the notion of standing before a vast congregation with a big floppy Bible in one hand and the other hand gesticulating to emphasise our point, we have to be practical. If your Bible is too big and hefty, you will certainly not be able to hold it in one hand while you preach. It will simply be too distracting. Depending on your church setting, it may also be too big to accommodate on the pulpit or lectern alongside your notes as well. Frankly, if you are relying on the weight of your Bible to convince people of the weight of your preaching, there are probably other issues to deal with anyway!

Not too small

Although this list may be starting to look like an excerpt from *Goldilocks and the Three Bears*, it is important to be practical. Even if your eyesight is very good, you may find that you still have to strain to focus on Bible print which is too small. The momentary loss of eye contact which this costs you with the congregation may be a price you are not willing to pay. Even if you have a favourite Bible which slips readily into a case or pocket, it may not be the best one from which to preach if it cannot be read at a distance.

Not too full

Some people's Bibles are like handbags with pages! Tucked inside their pages are everything from next week's shopping list and a receipt for coffee to notes on the theology of biblical inspiration. In particular, Christians tend to accumulate bookmarks with verses on, church notice sheets, and little pieces of paper with quotations from the Bible and elsewhere written on them. Of course, this is absolutely fine if it means that you can always find those things. A Bible crammed with all these additional items may well be the sign of a person who treasures their Bible. However, those additional items will only be a distraction when you preach. Either they will make it hard to prop the Bible open at the relevant page, or, worse still, they will detach themselves at some inopportune moment! Do you really want that bookmark with the fluffy duck on it, which amuses you so much, to float down to earth just as you are making your appeal to turn to Christ? If you want to use the same Bible for everything, make sure you ditch the junk before you take it into the pulpit.

Not too old

Connected with the above is the need to make sure that your Bible is not so old that it has turned into a kind of loose-leaf binder! I once had a Bible where, every time I opened it, two chapters of 2 Kings would waft gently down from the pulpit to the floor. The first time or two that it happened, it was funny, but thereafter it was a downright distraction. Either it made it almost impossible to find my place, or it took people's attention at just the wrong moment. You wouldn't expect your doctor to use a threadbare stethoscope with the earpieces hanging off just because it was his or her favourite, would you? If you want to keep your old 'loose-leaf' Bible because of its sentimental value, by all means do so – but don't preach from it!

Not too strange

Of course, there is a certain extent to which the Bible is strange no matter what you do with it. The Bible's words will always jar on the soul and jangle on our thoughts, because that is what they are meant to do. However, there is no point in *unnecessarily* emphasising the Bible's strangeness. Before you preach, either in your own church or elsewhere, try to find out which Bible version most people are using. This is important, because otherwise you may refer in your preaching to particular words and phrases in the text which the members of your congregation do not have before them. This may either sow confusion about what it really says, or sow doubt as to the basis of what you are saying. While it is quite possible to explain that you are using a different version, this can end up preoccupying the minds of preacher and listeners in an unhelpful way.

Not too translated

Despite what I have said about identifying with the Bible used by your congregation, there are still some versions which are best avoided when preaching. Within Bible translation, there are two key categories: formal equivalence and dynamic equivalence. Formal-equivalence translations aim for the highest calibre of literal word-for-word accuracy, without worrying too much about the readability of the finished product. The epitome of this style would be the *King James Version* in archaic English, and the *New American Standard Version* in modern English. Dynamic-equivalence translations, on the other hand, set a high premium on readability. Dynamic-equivalence translators have tried their utmost to understand the impact of the original text on its original audience, and then to reproduce that effect for today's readers. The best example of this today is *The Message*. We should be cautious, however, about how we use such dynamic-equivalence versions when preaching. If the text has already been translated from its original language, and then rephrased in contemporary language, and you then expound that rephrasing of the translation, the words have come a very long way since they were first written. Dynamic-equivalence translations are excellent for capturing the tone of a Bible passage, but do not lend themselves so easily to a verse-by-verse or word-by-word exposition.

The key advice throughout here is: choose your Bible with care!

A generous allocation of time

Like most skills, preparing a sermon will probably get quicker with practice. However, if it gets too quick, you should probably be worried! As we will see in the next chapter, the various stages of preparing the sermon mean that it is a process which should not be rushed. You must allow time for the Word to penetrate into your heart and mind. You must also allow time for your written word to play on your mind. I call this process 'percolation' – like the process in the kitchen where the rich flavour of the roasted coffee permeates the water and makes something drinkable. Often, a sermon which has been thought about on a Monday and written on a Tuesday will look quite different after it has percolated through to Friday. At that point, it will be amended or even rewritten. Different preachers will allow different amounts of time to write a sermon. Personally, I have rarely written a sermon in less than half a day. This should not surprise us. Writing a sermon is an act of creation – like painting a picture or carving a sculpture. Such things should not be rushed except in unusual circumstances – and it's usually possible to tell when they have been!

Preparing to preach

So, now you have chosen your venue, picked out your Bible, set aside your two pieces of paper and allowed yourself ample time. What now? At this point, it is easy to feel like an artist facing a blank canvas with a commission waiting, or a student staring at an empty page with a deadline looming. Don't panic! There are so many steps we could outline, but the following ten should be plenty to get started.

1. Pray

In fact, 'pray' should be the instruction as point 1a, 2a, 3a and so on, for it should infuse every single step of the preaching process. Prayerless sermons are not only powerless but also dangerous. However, in the interests of neatness, we shall place prayer here at point 1. To save you from meandering around in a state of uncertainty as to what to pray for, try using the guide below, based on your five senses.

Sight

Pray that God might enable you to see what the Bible really says to you on this occasion. This might not be the same as it said to you yesterday, or what it might say tomorrow. It might not be the same as it says to 1,000 other preachers in 1,000 other settings. What matters is what it says to you right here, right now as the person charged with speaking for God to a particular group of his people.

Sound

Pray that you might be sensitised to hear the needs of your congregation. These might be the kind of voices that say 'I'm afraid' or 'where is God?' or 'what does it mean?' God hears these voices all the time, and your prayer should be that on this occasion he allows you to hear the ones you really need to hear. In other words, you ask him to share some of his inside information with you as the preacher.

Smell

If you ever meet a really experienced sailor, or perhaps a farmer, that person will probably be able to tell you what the weather is up to just by sniffing the air. Over the years, their instinct has heightened their sense of smell to such an extent that they can 'read' the air in a way unknown to the rest of us. Pray that you might be able to 'sniff' those changes and movements in the spiritual atmosphere which indicate what the Holy Spirit is up to at this point in this place.

Taste

One of the reasons that Christ left us with the sacraments of bread and wine was to ensure that we had a touchable and tasteable reassurance of his ongoing presence. In the same way, pray that you might taste the presence of Christ with you – both in the quiet sanctuary of the study as you prepare, and later on the lonely pinnacle of the pulpit as you preach.

Touch

Lastly, you must pray that your study of the Bible, and the sermon you prepare from it, touch the lives of those who listen. The whole point of preaching is to allow God to touch hearts, minds and lives through the medium of his ancient Word and the contemporary human voice. In fact, as you pray this prayer, you may well find that it is not only those who listen, but also the one who speaks, who are touched by God.

2. Read the Bible

I have mentioned before my interest in the world of professional translation. As a translator prepares a piece of text for translation, he or she must read it with the utmost thoroughness in order to make sure they understand it. Without understanding what the text says, how it says it and what it does not say, the translator dare not embark on the process of rephrasing it in some other tongue. In order to do this, the translator will often pass the text through a series of 'filters' in order to really understand it. These filters can be of great service to the preacher too.

Genre

What is the genre of the text you are reading? At its most basic level, this might simply be the difference between Old Testament and New. The focus of the Old Testament is primarily communal, for example, while that of the New is more individual. Was each writer communicating bare facts, a set of instructions, a philosophical principle or a deeply felt emotion? You also need to ask to whether this is poetry or prose.

Cultural

Once the purpose of the text is ascertained, questions must be asked about the way it is communicated. Has the writer drawn on understandings and customs particular to his own culture, or borrowed from that of another? Is the writer's cultural background above or below the surface of the text? In Bible texts, this is particularly important, where there are cultural allusions to the world of the Bible. This might be an allusion to the Jewish sacrificial system in the Old Testament, for example. In the New, there might be a reference to Roman practices of slavery or military service invading the language of the text.

Tonal

Once the purpose and the cultural background of the text are clarified, you need to see if there is evidence of a particular tone at work. Does the writer choose a particular register for the piece, and if so does it imply anything about its source or its audience? This might include a particular social register or even a particular local bias in terms of dialect. The writer might also adopt a pejorative or an affirmative tone in the text.

Semantic

The word 'semantic' simply means 'meaning' – so look to see how the writer gets his meaning across. What semantic devices are at work in the text? Do the words used imply a particular attitude, either positive or negative? Has the writer included either direct or veiled references to other works of literature? The writer may use words with particular associated meanings (such as 'nurse' being associated with 'woman', and 'doctor' with 'man'), either deliberately or accidentally.

Formal

Subject the text now to even closer scrutiny. Check it at the grammatical level to see how the sentences fit together. Check it at the sentential level to see what the construction of each sentence tells us about the writer's intent. Check it at the lexical level, to see why particular words were chosen where another one would carry a similar meaning.

This may look like a lot of work, but it is there to ensure that your first reading of the Bible does not simply skate over the surface of the text. With time and experience, you will find yourself employing these filters without even noticing it.

3. 'Virgin' notes

You remember those two pieces of paper you set aside in the previous chapter? Take one of them now. At the head of the paper, you can either write 'hermeneutical', if you are feeling theological, or 'Bible' if you are not. Hermeneutics is the science of interpreting a source in order to derive its meaning, and draws its name from *Hermes*, the ancient Greek messenger of the Gods. On this piece of paper, you need to write down any insights or questions which struck you while you were reading the Bible text and passing it through the filters above. These are not the further insights you might gain by reading the commentaries, which we shall deal with under the next heading. Nor are they insights you might have on how to communicate your text, which will go later on your second piece of paper. No, these are virgin insights, unsullied by other people's opinions from the commentaries, or by concerns about how you might fashion the end product. They might be questions, one-word observations, or even verses which particularly struck you. It is quite possible that further stages of the sermon process will cause you to revise or expand these initial insights; but they are too precious to lose.

4. Commentary notes

Still on that first piece of paper, it's time to turn to the commentaries now, at which point you will have to make some choices. Of course, if you are new to preaching and are borrowing somebody else's library, the choice will be limited. If you are choosing commentaries for yourself, though, what should you look out for?

Beware of dinosaurs

All commentaries are expensive, and often the older ones can be bought cheaper second hand. However, be careful what you buy. Buying an old commentary, based on old scholarship, can be a false economy. Biblical scholarship, hermeneutical thinking and even the relevant discoveries in biblical archaeology may have moved on since the commentary was written. Some old commentaries are still available in modern covers, especially one-volume editions which cover the entire Bible. Their age does not mean that they are without value; but you should exercise caution. Matthew Henry's commentary, for example, is very popular. However, if people were aware that the author died in 1714, and if they saw the engravings of him with his powdered wig and his frock coat, they might be more cautious about applying his insights in the twenty-first century!

Horses for courses

There are all kinds of different Bible commentaries, from the scholarly to the devotional. Obviously, you will want to make use of those whose language and tone suit your particular mindset. Reading a commentary which either confuses or infuriates you will do little for your sermon preparation! However, you should be careful when using those commentaries which are designed largely as a devotional aid. The writers of these commentaries have put in the same kind of biblical research as is behind the more academic tomes, but they have gone one stage further and applied the Bible to the lives of the readers in the way which seems right to them. This is very helpful; but, for you as a preacher, it may short-circuit the process described above in the section on prayer. You may find yourself unduly swayed by their particular interpretation or application. If you do decide to use a devotional commentary, make sure that your critical faculties are in a high state of alert!

It's all Greek

One of the features which divides Bible commentaries is whether they are based on the original text of the Greek or Hebrew, or on its English translation. While it is possible to use a commentary based on the original-language version even if you haven't learnt that language, you may find it a frustrating process. Unless you have the opportunity to learn the biblical languages, you will probably find English-language versions much more helpful.

Balancing act

If at all possible, try to read commentaries from different theological perspectives. Whether your comfort zone is at the evangelical or the liberal end of the spectrum, try to read some commentaries from the opposite end. In the end, it will be up to you as a preacher whether you take a little, a lot or no notice of what these people say. However, it is good to be exposed to their different points of view in order to formulate your own opinion.

Most commentaries are written by biblical scholars who have tried their hardest to ascertain the original meaning of the text. In order to do so, they have combined linguistic skills with historical and theological understanding. However, they don't know your congregation or your context. Therefore, you must feel free to pick and choose from among their insights. Your hungry congregation does not want a tour of everyone's opinions about the Bible; they want you to help them make sense of it in their particular context.

5. Communication notes

Now it's time to set aside your 'Bible' piece of paper, and take the second piece. Just as you wrote 'Bible' or 'hermeneutical' at the head of that piece, so now you should write 'communication' or 'homiletics' at the head of this one. 'Homiletics' is the study of communicating with people and is the word from which we derive 'homily'. This sheet will probably end up quite messy by the time you are finished, but that's fine. As you turn over in your mind all the things you have written down on the first sheet, begin to consider how you might communicate them. You might write down key points, memorable quotes or even relevant stories. You might also note down here significant events and concerns in the lives of your congregation on which you expect this sermon to touch. The fact that you write them down here does not mean they will necessarily end up in the finished sermon; but they are part of the creative process. As themes, quotes, stories and illustrations begin to cover the paper, it can be helpful to draw lines between those which are connected. Thus, a sermon on Matthew 6:19:21, for example, may have the following:

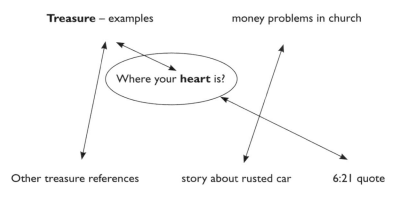

If we try to be too neat too soon, we can end up short-circuiting the creative process. At this stage, you should not reject any idea which could possibly be relevant, no matter how strange it might seem. There will be plenty of time to weed them out later. Having written these communication notes, the best thing to do is to get up and go away, out of your quiet study space. This might be for an hour or two, or you might have to leave it for a day or two. Either way, it allows these different ideas 'house room' in your mind, and will help you to sort out which ones should be kept and which ones should be rejected when you return to it. Before we move on, though, a word about this 'two-paper process'. It helps to prevent corrupting the hermeneutical process with the homiletical, or vice versa. In other words, it prevents you from spending all your time while reading the Bible by rushing ahead to think about how you will communicate it. On the other hand, it ensures that your thoughts about communication are not unduly dominated by what the commentaries and the scholars say.

6. Structured draft

Now that you have your Bible notes and your communication notes, and now that you have had time to think about them, it is time to order your thoughts. At this stage, I would refer you to the advice given to me by a theology lecturer many years ago when I was panicking about my first written assignment: 'tell me in one sentence what you want it to say'. Even with the most profound theological material in the world, it should still be possible to state clearly and concisely the purpose of the sermon. If you cannot state this as its preacher, what chance does the listener stand? Once you are clear about this aim, everything else in the process becomes subservient to it. It affects how you order your material, what sort of illustrations you use, the number and nature of any biblical quotations, and how the sermon ends and begins. The statement of the sermon's purpose might be very simple. For example, with the passage from Matthew quoted above, it might be any one of the following:

- Be careful what you treasure
- Hold onto the right things
- Heavenly hope and earthly possessions.

Often, preachers spend hours thinking up a sermon title which will be almost instantly forgotten, instead of devoting their time to honing a focus which will last throughout the sermon's length.

Now you have your guiding focus, begin to order your material. If you are going to divide your material up into different points, choose the order in which you will do so. Then insert under each heading the relevant verses and a note of the kind of thing you want to say. At this stage, nothing needs to be in full sentences, simply notes. Below is an example for our Matthew passage.

Focus statement: be careful what you treasure

- Introduction
- *Earthly things*: v. 19, vulnerable houses; v. 20, disappointment from earthly treasure
- *Heavenly things*: v. 20, value of things which last for ever
- *The heart*: how we feel about treasure – v. 21
- Conclusion.

This draft now gives you a 'grid' into which any supplementary material can be slotted.

7. Insert introduction, illustrations, biblical references and conclusion

At this point, you will need to refer to your communication/ homiletical sheet and see what material you will choose in order to serve the focus of the sermon. However, you need to exercise caution with all these elements of the sermon.

Introductions

Hook or hoax? It is hard to overemphasise the importance of the sermon's introduction. Your ability to grasp people's attention and whet their appetite in the first few seconds of preaching will determine the interest they accord you throughout what follows. The introduction should be a hook which grasps onto the listeners' lives and reels them in. However, make sure that it is not a hoax. It can be a hoax if it tells a funny or fascinating story which has absolutely nothing to do with what follows. To grasp people's attention with such an introduction is to gain it under false pretences. Avoid introductions, too, which promise something they can't deliver. A sermon introduction which promises to 'solve once and for all the problem of suffering', for instance, might gain lots of interest – but is unlikely to come up with the goods.

Illustrations

As we have said in chapter 'I', it is important to avoid illustrations which are either hopelessly out of date or offensive to your listeners. Avoid, also, a surfeit of illustrations which are personal. While they may have their place from time to time, your congregation is more concerned with learning about God than learning about you. Illustrations must illustrate something!

Biblical references

Depending on your church tradition, your congregation may expect you either to quote extensively from the passage on which you have preached, or not to mention it again once the reading is over. You will have to be guided by their expectations. However, it is wise to avoid quoting too extensively from other parts of scripture. Although this can build up a picture of the Bible's overall story, and avoid a piecemeal approach to scripture, it can be off-putting if we use it too much. It can either make the sermon very jerky and hard to follow, or leave the listener confirmed in his or her belief that only the preacher really knows what the Bible is all about. As we saw in chapter 'I', sermons should be illustrative of how to handle scripture, but this must be done gently so as to avoid losing people on the way.

Conclusions

Someone once said that the world will end 'not with a bang but with a whimper'. The same could be said of many sermons.

Some of them end their useful life long before the preacher stops speaking, and others seem to painfully and publicly run out of steam. Unless you are very experienced, you should plan in advance, under the guidance of the Holy Spirit, how the sermon will end. Of course, it is possible for that same Spirit to change it 'on the spot', but this will be the exception rather than the rule. Your purpose statement for the sermon will help you here. If its focus is to challenge, you will choose one kind of conclusion, whereas, if its focus is to comfort, you will choose another. Having chosen it, stick to it.

Our sample outline of the sermon on Matthew 6:19–21 might now look something like this:

Focus statement: be careful what you treasure

- *Introduction:* If you had to leave your house right now and never come back, with only a few minutes to grab a few possessions, what would they be? Such a moment would soon reveal what really matters to you.

- *Earthly things:* v. 19, vulnerable houses; v. 20, disappointment from earthly treasure. Story about the loss of a precious possession.

- *Heavenly things:* v. 20, value of things which last for ever. Overseas mission story on the value of eternal things when there are few possessions.

- *The heart:* how we feel about treasure – v. 21. Note how the gain and loss of treasure in the Old Testament reflects the people's relationship with God.

- *Conclusion:* most of us will not have to leave our houses for ever today, and living in a tent in the garden to *prove* our detachment from material possessions would be pointless. But would you be prepared to let go of something precious this week – even a prejudice or a dream – if God asked you to?

8. Mind your language!

Now that you have a detailed plan for the sermon, you need to read it through prayerfully. God gave us the gift of language. Somehow he created within us the miraculous process whereby ideas are converted into sound waves and back again. Think about it, even in this simple illustration of describing a beautiful view to a friend:

1. You see the view
2. That view forms pictures in your mind
3. You choose descriptive words in your mind
4. You speak those descriptive words by moving your mouth and generating sound waves
5. Those same sound waves strike your friend's ear drum
6. The ear drum sends signals to your friend's brain
7. Your friend's brain unscrambles those signals
8. Your friend forms pictures in his or her mind
9. Your friend describes how he or she feels about the pictures
10. The whole process starts again …

If that process is to take place several hundred times while you preach, it is worth choosing your words carefully. Think about evocative words and phrases. Make sure that questions are phrased clearly. Try to ensure that any allusions to other biblical passages are expressed so clearly that even a person who has not read them understands the point you are making. As a preacher, words are the tools of your trade – so choose them wisely!

9. Preaching notes

There are as many styles of notes as there are preachers. My own preference is for fairly full ones. There are two reasons for this. The first is that, when I began to preach, it was in a foreign language – French. In such a context, I did not dare to use anything less than full notes in case I slipped inadvertently into heresy! The second reason is that I am an extremely slow typist. This means that, by the time I have typed my notes, I have probably memorised most of them! You, of course, will adopt your own style. Here, however, are some points worth considering.

Paper size

While A4 notes give you plenty of room to set out your ideas, they can also be quite ungainly in the pulpit. On a small pulpit or lectern, it is easy to inadvertently nudge A4 notes over the edge, which can be embarrassing, and can cause you to pick them back up in the wrong order! The sight of a preacher taking a sheaf of A4 sheets out of his or her Bible and unfolding them carefully can cause the heart of many a listener to sink. Think about using A5 as a more manageable size. Alternatively, if your notes consist only of bullet points, then index cards might be fine.

Font size

Whichever size of paper you choose, make sure that you don't choose a font size which is too small to read. Notes which are easy to read in pitch 10 in the study may suddenly seem smaller in the pulpit! I would recommend 12 as a minimum, with possibly 14 for headings and special points.

Highlights

While every sermon should undoubtedly have its highlights, the use of highlighters in your notes can be useful too! I use a system of different colours to indicate Bible quotes, other quotes, questions and illustrations. While it does make my notes look very messy, it also helps me to find my place easily if I get distracted or carried away. Ease of navigation is probably more important than beauty of presentation anyway!

Page numbering

This may seem like a really obvious point, but it is worth taking the time to number the pages of your notes. The few minutes it takes you will really pay dividends if your drop your Bible or knock the notes off the lectern. Although you may think that you know your material so well that the order will be obvious, it might not seem like that in the heat of the moment.

10. Pray and leave it

Now that you have gone through this process of praying, reading, listening and writing, the best thing you can do with your sermon is to leave it. Pray *about* it, by all means, but don't pray *through* it. Any prayer time between now and when you preach should be devoted to praying for you as a preacher and your congregation as listeners. If you pray with the text of your sermon notes open in front of you, the temptation to fiddle with them will be almost overwhelming. Let God worry about the preaching for now – you worry about the preacher!

When you preach

Now, all that preparation is behind you. Ready or not, the time has come to preach. Before you now is a group of people, either large or small, hungry to hear from God. By coming to church, they have declared their belief that God has something to say to them, and their desire to do something about it. As you look at them now, perhaps they look like hungry chicks in the nest – opening and shutting their mouths as a plea for food, and wanting to grow. Right now, it is your job to feed them. This is not because you are more special or more holy or more important than a single one of them. Instead, it is because you have been appointed and anointed by God to meet their needs on this particular occasion. How will you fare?

Ride your nerves

You may be surprised that I don't say to ignore your nerves. After all, nerves are born of fear, and the Bible tells us that 'perfect love casts out fear' (1 John 4:18). However, your nerves are a useful reminder of your weakness and of the reliance on God which you must therefore show. Not only this, but, as many sportspeople and actors will tell you, the adrenalin which gives you that nervous feeling can also be used to enhance your 'performance' and release your best skills and abilities. I have often said that the day I stop feeling nervous as I approach the pulpit is the day I will stop preaching. My nerves act as a salutary reminder to me that I cannot do this alone. In fact, deeper than that, they remind me that I dare not presume to feed these people from my own meagre resources. If I did, they would pretty soon starve! Yield your nerves to God, by all means. Ask him to help you make the best use of them. But don't, whatever you do, ask him to take them away completely. They are the preacher's safety belt – strapping you firmly to God for the ride ahead!

Bow your heart

Remember that feeling of humility we discussed in the chapter on 'Before you preach'? We talked about Jesus' reassuring words that 'apart from me you can do nothing' (John 15:5). Right now, you need to make sure that this is your final thought before entering the pulpit. A minute or two dwelling on those words will do more to empower your sermon than ten minutes reading back through your notes again. As preachers, we are servants to many. We are servants to the incarnate Word – to Jesus himself. We are servants to the written word – the Bible. Also, we are servants to the people who have gathered to hear us preach. We are not there to impress them or to frighten them, or even to jolly them along. We are there to create a space where they can encounter God and his living Word. This is a great honour, and a humbling task.

Keep your gaze

If God felt that the written word was all that was needed, he would not call men and women as preachers. If he thought that a weekly portent or miracle on a Sunday morning would be sufficient, again the preachers would be redundant. However, that is not the way he chooses to do it. This is because he is the God of the incarnation. He is the one who came up with the idea of turning his Word into flesh so that people like you and me could relate to it. I say 'you and me' without knowing a thing about you. However, I do know that you have a heart, and a soul, and eyes to see. When we engage in this 'incarnate' form of communication, it is vital that we maintain good eye contact with the people to whom we preach. After all, this is fundamental to human communication. When you first begin to preach, you may find the whole business of eye contact very disconcerting. You may feel that people are staring at the spot of breakfast you failed to wash off your cheek, or seeking to communicate some unspoken approval or disapproval to you. Resist the temptation to lose your concentration by interpreting every facial gesture you observe. After all, you might be quite wrong! Avoid, too, the 'nodding dog' approach – where you simply sweep your gaze from one side of the congregation to the other like one of those toy dogs on the parcel shelf of a car. When you first start, you may find it helpful to pick a spot in the air just above the back row and focus on it. With time, though, you will relax into a more natural form of eye contact with your congregation. You may even learn to enjoy this collection of faces. After all, etched into them is a story of human endeavour and God's faithfulness which has to be worth reading!

Watch your, um, pace

When speaking in public, one of the most natural inclinations in the world is to speed up the pace of our delivery without even noticing it. This may be simply brought on by nerves, or there may be other factors at work. It may indicate our sense of urgency that these important truths must be communicated RIGHT NOW and there is not a second to spare. You may feel embarrassed that you have too much material and wish to cover this up by rushing through it. Try to resist these feelings. If there is too much material, then you can adjust your approach next time you preach. However, for now, it is better to deliver what you have researched and ordered so carefully with the confidence that befits a spokesman or spokeswoman of God. Which brings me to the curse of the *er* ... or the *um* ... or even the *kinda*. When we insert these interjections into our every phrase or sentence, it has two principal effects. The first is to irritate those who listen to us. Secondly, they will probably end up taking more notice of these interjections than they do of the real message we wish to convey. The same thing happens when we engage unconsciously in 'upspeaking', or raising the note of our voice at the end of every sentence. It has the effect of making every sentence feel like a question, and making the congregation feel that we are unsure of our material. As we shall see in our final chapter, it is very unlikely that you will notice these things for yourself, so you will have to find another way of detecting them, so that you can then do something about it.

Enjoy your humanity

I remember distinctly one Sunday when a church member whose work had kept him from church arrived during the last hymn. At the door, he shook my hand and announced with a grin that this was the best sermon he had ever heard me preach. It took me a minute to realise what he had said, and then I threw back my head and laughed. Sometimes, we preachers take ourselves far too seriously! Because you are human, there are some days when your carefully planned sermon will go down a storm, and others when it will appear to die somewhere between the pulpit and the pew. On occasions, you will feel that the congregation are with you, hanging on every word. On others, it may seem like they are merely tolerating your presence while waiting to do something more interesting. As your preaching experience lengthens, you will see every emotion pass across their faces – from peace to sorrow and back again – just as they will on yours. This, however, is the joy of being human. As intelligent and articulate creatures, we are designed to communicate through words and ideas. As imperfect creatures, we are bound to find that sometimes we do it well and sometimes we do it poorly. It is precisely this kind of challenge which makes preaching more than a job – it is a calling. As a human being with a particular gift, you are called to put it to service in the best way and for the highest purpose. I am absolutely certain that I have preached plenty of sermons which make me cringe with embarrassment, and have done the same thing to the poor souls who had to listen to them! I am equally certain that, along the way, God has taken my very ordinary words and ideas and done something extraordinary with them. As a preacher, you should enjoy your humanity for all it is worth – not despite its flaws, but because of them.

Trust God

The main thing to remember when you are preaching, as we saw in chapter 'T', is that you do so in partnership with God. The preacher is not a brave champion, sent out alone onto the battlefield to do battle while God watches from the sidelines. Rather, he or she is a co-worker with God, acting in his strength and blown along by the warm breath of his Spirit. If you entered into your preparation for preaching with the right heart, and gave your best efforts to understanding the Bible and communicating it, your efforts will

not be in vain. Remember the words of Isaiah, a man who quaked
with fear at the very thought of speaking up for God when he was
first asked to do so:

> As the rain and the snow come down from heaven
> And do not return to it without watering the earth
> And making it bud and flourish
> So that it yields seed for the sower and bread for the eater
> So is my word that goes out from my mouth
> It will not return to me void
> But will accomplish what I desire
> And achieve the purpose for which I sent it.
>
> (Isaiah 55:10–11)

Those words have been a comfort to every preacher since Isaiah
first wrote them down in the seventh century BC, and they should
be to you as well.

After you preach

The study door is closed – you won't go in there until next week at the earliest. The church door is closed too – the lights are off and everyone has gone home. You have delivered your sermon as the product of your thought and labour and prayer and study. What now? It is important to recognise your own feelings as a preacher on the one hand, and the feelings of the congregation on the other.

Your feelings

Elation

As you step down from the pulpit, and the adrenalin begins to ebb away, you will probably feel elated. This is not an 'unspiritual' reaction, and should be of no surprise to you. After all, you have worked and prayed and worried about this event for some time – so why should you not feel glad that you have completed it? Not only this, but also as a Christian you should always feel a degree of satisfaction when you know you have completed a task which God gave you to do. We see this in the life of Nehemiah, as he takes a last look back at the tasks he has fulfilled. 'Remember me with favour, O my God' (Nehemiah 13:31). We see it in Jesus' story of the talents, where the reward for a job well done is the sound of the master's voice saying: 'well done, good and faithful servant' (Matthew 25:23). Of course, you have done this particular task with his help. His Spirit has inspired you and his strength has enabled you. That does not mean, however, that you should not feel a warm glow that you have done what you were called to do.

Exhaustion

As more of the adrenalin ebbs away, the physical exhaustion will begin to affect you more. Not only your throat, but probably your arms and legs will feel tired too. The experience of soaking up people's undivided attention, and giving your all in order to maintain it, is bound to take it out of you. Knowing that this is the case makes it easier to deal with. When you are new to preaching, try to ensure that you are not kept too long at the church after the service is over. Also, be good to yourself in the hours following the church service. Don't do too much, and certainly nothing that demands too much cerebral or mental power. There are many different kinds of tired. Some are good, and some are draining and bad. However, the tiredness which comes from a job well done in the service of the King takes some beating!

Deflation

As your body begins to recover, you may find that it is your mind and spirit which begin to flag instead. After all, you have looked forward to this moment. Since the day you first felt that God was calling you tentatively into the preaching ministry, you have devoted time, effort and prayer to the enterprise. Even if you have another preaching opportunity booked on the horizon, this particular one is still over. Like an actor after the curtain has fallen, or a sprinter after the finishing tape is broken, you will feel an overwhelming sense that this particular event is over. The feeling is a strange one, since it combines elements of sadness and joy. The best thing is to recognise it for what it is. It is not depression, it is not chronic fatigue, it is not evidence of spiritual oppression – it is simply a reaction to an event of high significance in your life.

Self-doubt

Despite what we have said above, there may be a moment at which natural deflation slips into something more corrosive. In the immediate aftermath of the sermon, you may find yourself beset with doubts about whether you did your best and whether God really spoke through you at all. While some of these questions are helpful, and can be dealt with at a later stage, they can also be a cynical ploy on the devil's part to bring you down as a preacher. Remember that God sets higher store by faithfulness than fruitfulness. Because of this, the lack of any obvious response to the sermon should not add to your self-doubt. The key question for you is not whether the sermon 'worked', but whether *you* did. In other words, did you do everything in your power to present God with a tool he could use for his purposes? If you did, then your spirit can rest assured. Even if you felt there was more you could have done, this can be turned to your advantage as you plan the next sermon. The best response to the devil's question about whether you did your best is probably:

> Of course not – I'm a sinner. Did *you* do *your* best?

Hunger

Unless you and others really misheard God about your call to preach, the next feeling you are likely to feel after all those above have subsided is hunger. In the first instance, this will be a hunger to put whatever it is you were preaching about into practice. There is nothing quite like preaching on a great theme to make you feel you should take some notice of it! Whether your theme was a call for deeper prayer or a challenge to give away more money, or even a reassurance about God's mercy, you will probably find yourself more hungry to heed it than any of your listeners. This can only be a good thing. The other kind of hunger you will feel is a hunger to preach again. If the experience of preaching, even with all its demands and hurdles, has made you feel alive and useful in the hands of God, there will be a hunger gnawing deep in your soul to do it again as soon as the opportunity presents itself.

Their feelings

Sometimes, the congregation will make you aware of their feelings even as you preach. Blank faces and glazed expressions have a way of getting through to you even when you are busy! Equally, there is a look of captivation, joy and heavenly hope which every preacher hopes to see on the faces of the congregation at least once in a lifetime. Remember: when you see these things as the one person standing at the front of the church, you occupy a uniquely privileged position. It can be a real thrill to see the power of God's Word at work live. After the sermon is over, some people will let you know immediately at the church door how they feel about what you said. These can range from the bland 'thank you, preacher' to a query on biblical history and theology, or a vehement attack on your sermon. Don't be too taken in by these comments, though.

The story is told of a young preacher visiting a church and standing at the door beside the resident minister after the service was over. As people filed past with smiles and handshakes, the visiting preacher was surprised to see one man come back again and again. Each time, he looked at the ground, rather than meeting the preacher's eyes, and muttered some criticism or other. When the visitor asked his host about the man, he replied airily: 'don't take any notice of him, he just repeats what he hears from other people'!

Any comments expressed immediately the service is over should be treated with caution! Instead, it is the more considered feeling which should concern us.

Encouragement

Many preachers genuinely struggle to believe that their sermon will encourage anybody. They shake their heads and say 'no, not me, not my sermon'. While this is done in the name of modesty, it can end up as insulting to God. If God chose you, if he heard your prayers for help and inspired your preparation and empowered your delivery – why should people *not* be encouraged? When I first started to hear these positive comments in response to my preaching, I found them extremely hard to bear. I didn't want to hear them because I was afraid they would mess with my head and inflate my ego. Those fears, however, were my problem, rather than being anything to do with the kind souls who wanted to thank their preacher. The best thing to do is to thank the person who is encouraged, to acknowledge that God's Word is a wonderful thing, and then to take both the comments and the feelings they generate within you into the private place of prayer.

Confusion

Occasionally, people may be genuinely confused by what you have said. This may be because you expressed it badly, in which case you will need to reconsider how you phrase it another time. Equally, they may be confused because the theological subject matter you chose is a difficult one. Any sermon on suffering, for instance, is bound to leave some ragged ends. A sermon on predestination could cause some confusion, even with the clearest explanation in the world. (I will resist the temptation to say it is *bound* to!) The important thing to recognise here is that your responsibility does not end as soon as the sermon is over. If you really care about the things you have said, rather than just enjoying the experience of saying them, you will need to find a way of helping those who struggle with them still. Of course, it may not be you who offers the help. Particularly if you are a visiting preacher, you may need to refer those who are confused to their own pastor or minister. If you know that the subject matter of your sermon is likely to puzzle a few minds or prick a few consciences, it may be worth organising some people who are prepared to offer prayer and listening with individuals after the service is over.

Self-doubt

As much as the preacher is prone to self-doubt, so is the listener. If you ask yourself whether you spoke as well you could, the listener may well ask whether they listened as hard as they could. If you ask yourself whether you gave God your all as you spoke, the listener may well ask whether they gave God their all as they listened. They may end up like Isaiah saying 'I am a sinner' (Isaiah 6:5), or like Peter's congregation on Pentecost day saying 'what shall we do?' (Acts 2:37). When you encounter this kind of response, the best approach to take is a horizontal one. By this, I mean that you need to reassure the listener that you and they are on level ground. You may have been the one preaching the sermon, but you are just as responsible for putting it into practice as they are. The response to the sermon is a shared responsibility, where both preacher and listener must answer to God. If either has not preached or listened as hard as they can, the only way is up!

Onward steps

Assess your own performance

Now that the immediate aftermath of the sermon is over, it is time for you to make a more sober assessment of how it went. Start off with the easy questions about whether you could make sense of your notes and whether you covered all the material you intended to. Look through the notes before you file them away by way of a reminder. Were you aware of God speaking through you, or did you feel that your own personality and opinions intruded more than you had intended them to? If at all possible, obtain a recording of the sermon. Having done so, sit down with a blank sheet of paper and make notes while you listen. Did you notice anything about the pace of its delivery? Were there particular phrases repeated lots of times? Were you afflicted by the curse of the *erm*? Though awkward and embarrassing, even with an audience of one, noticing these things can help you to avoid them on subsequent occasions. It is also worth researching various 'instruments' available from different organisations to help you assess your sermon in a structured way.

Enlist the help of others to assess your performance

Depending upon your particular personality, you may find it easier to go through the exercise mentioned above with the help of one or two trusted friends. If you are intending to do so, then it would be wise to alert those friends before the sermon is preached. That way, they will pay a particular kind of attention when they are listening to you preach. You may find it helpful to give them a set of questions to consider as they listen. Below are two examples:

Question set 1

- what was the sermon's form? (argument, story, poetic etc.)
- what was the sermon's function? (what was it trying to achieve?)
- what was its focus? (what was its enduring image or challenge?)

Question set 2

- what did you hear? (words, images or ideas)
- what did you feel? (encouraged, challenged etc.)
- what added to or subtracted from the value of the sermon?

If you are going to embark on this shared exercise, it is important that all participants are clear about its purpose. It is not about your value as a person, but about your skills as a preacher. Its short-term goal is to help you preach better, and its long-term goal is to form Christlike Christians as they hear an authentic Word of God. You may well find that the group of friends who provide this feedback for you become your trusted prayer partners too, praying for you in sermon preparation as well as helping you to reflect on delivery.

Keep going

As you look ahead, either to the next sermon or to the next few years of preaching, commit yourself to excellence. To preach is to serve the King – and he deserves your best. Learn where you can, change where you should – and never, never doubt the wisdom of the one who called you.

I could leave you with the words of Isaiah the prophet about the preaching of good news (Isaiah 52:7). I could leave you with Paul's advice to Timothy to preach the good news 'in season and out of season' (2 Timothy 4:2). Both passages are words to cherish. Instead, I leave you with the words of a storybook vicar from a little book entitled *Postman Pat's Rainy Day*. As water leaks through the church roof on a rainy day, he asks the postman to put the letters in the pulpit – 'no drips in there', he says. Long may his words be true!

Bibliography

Barth, Karl, *The Preaching of the Gospel* (Westminster Press, 1961).

Brueggemann, Walter, *Finally Comes the Poet: Daring Speech for Proclamation* (Minneapolis: Fortress Press, 1989).

Craddock, Fred, *Preaching* (Nashville: Abingdon Press, 1985).

Cunliffe, John, *Postman Pat's Rainy Day* (Southam: Scholastic, 1982).

Dawkins, Richard, *The Selfish Gene* (Oxford: Oxford University Press, 2006).

Day, David, *Embodying the Word: A Preacher's Guide* (London: SPCK, 2005).

Graves, Mike, *The Fully Alive Preacher* (Louisville: WJKP, 2006).

Hawks, Tony, *One Hit Wonderland* (London: Ebury Press, 2007).

Jones, Kirk Byron, *The Jazz of Preaching* (Nashville, Abingdon Press, 2004).

Littledale, Richard, *Stale Bread? A Handbook for Speaking the Story* (Edinburgh: Saint Andrew Press, 2007).

Long, Thomas G., *The Witness of Preaching* (Louisville: WJKP, 1989).

Lowry, Eugene, *The Homiletical Plot* (Atlanta: John Knox Press, 1978).

Marguerat, Daniel and Yvan Bourquin, *How to Read Bible Stories* (London: SCM Press, 1999).

Miller, Calvin, *Spirit, Sword and Story* (Michigan: Baker Books, 1996).

Miller, Calvin, *The Sermon Maker* (Grand Rapids: Zondervan, 2002).

Mitchell, Jolyon, *Visually Speaking* (Louisville: WJKP, 1999).

Otto, Rudolf, *The Idea of the Holy* (Oxford: Oxford University Press, 1923).

Schlafer, David, *Your Way with God's Word* (Boston: Cowley, 1995).

Schlafer, David, *Playing with Fire: Preaching Work as Kindling Art* (Minnesota: Cowley, 2004).

Sheppard, Jackie, *Beyond the OHP: Using Technology in Church* (Milton Keynes: Authentic Lifestyle, 2003).

Tidball, Derek, *Builders and Fools* (Leicester: IVP, 1999).

Tisdale, Leonora Tubbs, *Preaching as Local Theology and Folk Art* (Minneapolis: Fortress Press, 1997).

Tozer, A. W., *Leaning into the Wind* (Eastbourne: Kingsway Publications, 1985).

Troeger, Thomas, *Imagining a Sermon* (Nashville: Abingdon Press, 1990).

Willimon, William, *Peculiar Speech: Preaching to the Baptized* (Grand Rapids: Eerdmans, 1992).